Diary of a Madman:

The musings, thoughts, philosophies, and

Observations of Jaysen True Blood

Book 2: The letters, FB replies, FB posts and unpublished thoughts

Part 1

By Jaysen True Blood

Cover photo by Rusty Cosworth

Foreword

═══

I have never claimed to know much of anything. In fact, I have always stated that I know very little and am always learning. It is this philosophy that has kept me pushing at the books and writing as if there was no tomorrow. It is also why I began the blog *Deep thoughts and Philosophies,* a totally nonfiction blog that I used as a springboard for my deepest discoveries and every eureka moment I have had in the past three and a half years.

Ironocally, I have had some who have disagreed or used a misinterpretation of a word or two to attempt a few "gotcha" moments only to find that I had already thought of that. In the pursuit of the truth, I have also learned that we have to let go of the notion that certain books are complete and that there is no other knowledge or wisdom that exists beyond them...a common pitfall of nearly every Christian I have ever met.

My eureka moment, where this realization was concerned, was when the minister at the church I was attending made the statement-as he held up the Bible-that the Bible was not complete. As a result, I went in search of whatever was missing. What I found was that if you wished to understand the context of something, you first had to be a student of the mythology, culture, and history of the region it was written.

This led me to realize that what I had been taught as "absolute" wasn't as absolute as we thought. It also made me realize that many of the "laws" we held so precious were rooted more in the philosophy of solidifying control of a loose alliance of people through separation from both their origin and through separation from those peoples they were emerging among or leaving behind.

At the same time, I realized that many things I had been taught were simply not so. It was this realization, and others, I began trying to put into words. Yes, the process has been painfully slow. But, ultimately , it has been rewarding. The following book is a collection of observations, letters never sent, philosophical musings, and deep thoughts that I have collected over 20 years. There is no reason to the rhyme, so they might seem a bit disconnected. This is because I am starting with the earliest and working my way to the present day.

Depending on how well received this book is, and how much time I have left in life at the present, I may make a second at a later date. Please bear with me, this is my first-and possibly only-nonfiction (non-poetry/lyric) work.

~Jaysen, 2017~

While You Were Out[2005]

While you were out:

I spent three hours applying for jobs.

In those three hours:

1. I made over a dozen contacts.
2. I got my foot into at least a dozen doors
3. And have a possible chance to do something different.

Out of those dozen:

1. I am sure that I will hear from at least half
2. Two that want more info have already contacted me.

A breakdown of those dozen:

1. Three were contract jobs.
2. A couple will only last a month.
3. One was for a writer.
4. Three were for show hosts.
5. But most were for actors or extras.
6. And most will last for 6 months or longer.
7. But all will get me out of your home.

If you do not consider these to be work opportunities:

You will never be happy with anything I will try to do. This is because I refuse to work for Eaton's. I *know* that I do not have what it takes to work there, I wouldn't last a day. I will not work at a job that will destroy my health. I am not built for that kind of work, anyway. And I do know, beyond a shadow of a doubt, what my limitations are. Besides, I have applied there numerous times and been rejected...just as I have applied to nearly every business in this area, without success. They just won't hire me.

To recap:

I am not, nor have I ever been lazy. Every job I have had, I have worked my ass off trying to keep it and never complained. I have always dealt honestly with every potential employer, never telling them that I knew how to do something when I did not. I admitted truthfully, when asked, that given my "druthers", I would rather not make such jobs a lifelong career, but that I was-in the same breath-hopeful that they would last me until something better came along. I was content to work at those places for as long as I had to wait for the better opportunity to come my way.

Often, I have had to settle for jobs that paid less than my labor was worth. These are, and always will be, just like any and all factory jobs—a dead end job. You cannot go any higher than what you start at. Seniority no longer means anything in the workplace. It won't secure you the next level higher anymore. It's just a number like your age or IQ. And often, these jobs don't last. If the management can find a way to cut you out of the line, they will. It doesn't matter if you have given them your all. How hard you work don't mean shit to them. If they can find someone less motivated than you, or cheaper to maintain than you, they will get rid of you. Work ethic don't mean jack to them. I know. I have been on the other end of this to be so naive as to think otherwise.

I can no longer afford to lose something right after I have found it. I need something that I know will be there and not have to worry about losing what I have been hired to do. Acting and being an extra is just that kind of job. They call on you because they need you. They aren't interested in letting you go because of financial distress within the company or because they have found someone cheaper. They state how much they're willing to pay, and if you want the job, you agree to it.

I am sorry that I cannot be another you, but my heart (nor God) would ever forgive me. I cannot go around being thought of as an asshole...and, unfortunately, that is what people see when they encounter you. I don't know how many jobs I have been refused because I admitted to being your son (and proudly, for a time). Every time, the look said it all—'oh, so you think we'd hire an asshole, huh?'—never mind the fact that I work hard and don't complain. Never mind that I am a separate individual. Never mind that I am not, nor ever will be, Alfred Delano Peterman. All they could see was that my dad was an asshole, so I must be one as well.

You see, the father's reputation *does* follow the son. But i used to stick up for you.indeed, I once had infinite respect for you. I looked up to you. But, like everything else someone tries to do for you, you destroyed it with your mouth. Your inability to shut up long enough to observe what's really going on around you in the world-or even listen to the truth-has destroyed everything. You don't see because you don't *want* to see. You don't hear because you don't want to listen. You believe that you know everything there is to know about getting a job, but you haven't had to go out and search for over 28 years. Things change. What was doable then isn't doable now. What could be said then is unspeakable now. You can't go and tell them the truth, yet you can't lie to them either. It's a *catch 22*. Damned if you do, damned if you don't. Honesty has lost ground out there. If you're too honest, they won't hire you. At the same time, if you omit something, or neglect to mention something thinking that it'll get you the job and they hire you only to find that you weren't totally honest, you get fired. You see, getting a job nowadays is a lot harder than it used to be.

You can go apply at several place that claim they're hiring, but that doesn't mean that you'll be the one they hire. You can be clean shaven, hair so short that people think you're bald, nicely dressed, and all...but none of that matters anymore. They don't care about your appearance unless you are going to be dealing with the public...and even then, they may not be concerned. Now, they look at age. If you're not a certain age, you don't get the job. Weight also applies here. As does a lot of other factors like who you know, who you're related to, or who you'll have sex with. If you don't have the connections or are too honorable to compromise your principles, then you don't get the job. Rarely do they deviate from this system.

Another thing that counts against you is whom you have worked under if, indeed, you've worked at a certain place before (that is why Vogel's has never hired me back. I worked there under Bill Shirley when I was with them the first time.). And, of course, there is the subject of past work record. Where you have worked, what you have done, if you've been laid off, fired, or quit does count. Of course, there are those who can talk their way into a job that they don't intend on keeping. And then, there are those of us who have trouble just getting our feet in the door when we want and need a job. Then, when we get it, we are the first to be let go even though we actually need the income. We are the ones who find ourselves jobless for a lot longer than we care to be.

Now...let's take a look at the ways you once suggested that I use to get a job.

Approach #1: demand the job; tell them to give you a job, then tell them why they should hire you and not the 'other guy'.

Reaction: Most employers will laugh you right out of their office. If they don't, they immediately call security and have you forcefully removed. They never give you a chance to get beyond step #1. They aren't stupid...and they aren't looking for assholes. In fact, they don't have any use for assholes. They already have a big enough supply of such people in their offices. They're called 'senior staff'.

Approach #2: wear a suit and tie to the interview.

Reaction: Most employers in the warehousing and manufacturing business don't care what you look like. They see you in a suit and wonder if you've lost your mind. Who, in their right mind, wears a suit and tie on an assembly line? No, the only time it is appropriate to wear such attire to an interview is if you are applying for an office job.

Approach #3: short hair, clean appearance.

———————

REACTION: GRANTED, like the suit and tie, there are interviews that call for this, but more often than not, appearance isn't super important. I, personally, have seen my share of times where—even though I was 'clean cut'—the scraggly person behind me or in front of me got the job and I didn't.

As I stated earlier, honesty will only get you so far nowadays. Most of the time, it will be a preventative factor where getting a job is concerned. Men of integrity are seemingly disliked. You show an honest bone in your body and they will try to corrupt you. If you resist and refuse, they try to get rid of you. Most times, though, you won't even get your foot in the door. You have to be world-wise enough to understand this. You can't just go out and expect to win a job. This isn't the lottery. You don't pick a number, then wait for them to call it. This isn't bingo. Nor is it a user-friendly time.

I can gladly state that I have never, I repeat *never,* (in my short life) lied to get a job. I have never promised things that I knew I could never carry out either. Make no promises, tell no lies, learn all you can, do what you know you can do. These are what I have always followed when I go to a job or to find a job. They are great maxims to live by, but they don't always get you the job. Indeed, every job I have had, I've gone into with the idea of learning all that I could. never have I ever stated 'yes, without a doubt, can I do that'. I knew, all too well, that if I failed I was fired. So all I could ever tell them was 'I can try' or 'I can learn'. I have always been willing to learn. It's the only way to survive. I have never turned away work that demanded me to learn something new. In fact, I have always welcomed it. This is one of the reasons why I try things that no one in the family has ever tried. Because I want to learn things.

Now, I must move on to the next thing on my mind. It is something that I have addressed earlier in passing. It is this erroneous idea that I am lazy. As you have read, I work hard when given a chance. But when it comes right down to it, we can only do what God wills us to do. Before we were born, He already knew what he wanted us to do. Some, He put to the plow. Some, He put to labor in factories. Some, He gave the talent for art. Some, He made to entertain. Some, to be musicians. Other to be bankers, lawyers, politicians, doctors, business types, and so on. In other words, we weren't created to be the same things. We were never meant to be clones of our parents. Nor were we all meant to follow their footsteps. We all have our own paths to follow. We mustn't judge another based on what our work may be. Nor should we be concerned with the world's view of us or our children.

With this said, I must now ask a question. Are you so untrusting of God that you must try to make His decisions for him? Must you make yourself God and sit in judgment, condemning any who do not measure up to your standards? Must you always be worried about what others may think of you because of me? Or are you willing to take that first step in complete and total faith and let God decide things for a change? (I know there was more than one question, but they have all been bugging me for a while.)

God, alone, knows what He wants us to do. Sometimes, we agree with Him. But sometimes, we think that *we* know best and try to impose our will onto those around us. When we do what wwe want, we ignore Him and show Him that we don't really love Him.

With some of us, He places us where we are supposed to be immediately. Some, He takes His time. Others may wait a lifetime. One never knows. But we must remain patient through it all. We must understand that God cannot and will not be rushed. He will do what He knows is right *in His own time.* He will do what needs to be done when it is time, no sooner and no later. If we make decisions counter to His will, then we suffer the consequences of our actions.

Sometimes, these can be found in a hastily found job, a marriage, or a wrong career choice just to name a few. Sometimes we get stuck working somewhere we weren't supposed to work and He just leaves us there because we still don't want to listen to Him. We want to be in control. But we aren't in control. He is.

And He always will be because He knows best. We, of and by ourselves, have no power whatsoever. We are weak. We know nothing apart from that which He reveals to us. And we only do that which He wills.

Sometimes, He just wants us to stop for a while and realign our thinking back to His. But some are too stubborn to understand this. They are too stuck on themselves, their own way of thinking, that nothing gets through to them. But when we stop and rest,sometimes in the quiet of our hearts, we can hear Him talking to us. When we stop doing and start listening, we begin to learn what He truly desires from us and where He wants us to go.

I could no more do your job than you could do mine. I could no more survive your life than you could mine.neither of us were meant to do the other's job. We can only do what we were meant to do. Do not try to impose expectations upon me. I will never be able to fulfill such a task.

I don't do anything anymore for the money. To pursue such a path is futile. Solomon said it best: "do not overwork to be rich; because of your own understanding, cease! Will you set your eyes on that which is not? For riches certainly make themselves wings; they fly away like an eagle toward Heaven." And christ, too, said it best with: "therefore, I say unto you do not worry worry about your life, what you will eat nor what you will drink; nor about your body, what you will put on..." indeed, we cannot add anything to ourselves by worrying. All this does is make us into monsters, savage little inhuman beasts, that lose sight of what is truly important. If it is God's will that gain monetary wealth, so be it. But I am not going to take matters into my own hands and force the issue. It may be His will that I remain poor, I don't know. But as Christ said: "put not up for yourselves treasures in this world where moth and rust destroy, and thieves break in and steal; but rather, set up for yourselves treasures in Heaven where moth and rust cannot destroy nor thief steal. For where your treasure is, so is your heart."

No, I don't do what I do for the money. For if I did, I would already be dead. Nor do I do it for the fame, power, or recognition. I could personally care less about such things. Besides, If God wants such things for me, then that is His choice. Nor do I do it because it is what you or any other human being wants of me. Your desires matter little to me. Your approval matters little to me. In fact, you opinion of me matters little to me.

I do what I do because it is what God wants me to do. I do what I do because I like doing what pleases God. i only look to God for approval or disapproval. I trust His judgment fully and completely. I know beyond a shadow of a doubt that He will never lead me wrong. Let me down, or impose impossible tasks upon me. He will enable me to do anything He wills me to do. Moreover, He will put me to doing what He has set for me to do. He, alone, will set me on the right path.

In my short life, I have come to realize that I cannot provide anything through my own power. I cannot supply anything I need. I can do *nothing*. I have no power of my own.

I cannot do anything unless it is God's will that I do it...even when it is seemingly of my own desire to do, or I give in to pressure, but these are usually object lessons from which I must learn. He provides all things. He, alone, takes care of our needs. He will see is through all. He, and He alone, deserves our praise. In Him, alone, should we place our trust and faith.

I have come to realize that I, in all fairness and love-for we are commanded to love-cannot judge anyone justly or rightly. This prevents me from condemning as well. I realize that these offices belong solely to God...not to you, not to me, nor to anyone else on this planet.we do not have the right to say what we do not know as fact. Gossip is not Gospel. Gossip betrays with its lies and insinuations, while Gospel lifts up with the truth.

I have also come to realize that it doesn't matter what men think, but rather, what God knows to be true about us. Our ego means absolutely nothing in light of the truth. It doesn't matter at all. I am not concerned with realizing my own selfish ambitions or desires anymore.

Yes, there are things I want to do, but the thing that matters is what God wants me to do. Perhaps you ought to review, with an open mind lacking any forethought as to what you wish to get out of them, the following verses: Luke 6: 35-37; Proverbs 23: 4 & 5; I Peter 5: 6 & 7; Galatians 5: 16-26; Ecc. 7: 8; II Timothy 2: 24; I Peter 3: 8 & 9; John 13: 34; Deut. 8: 18; Proverbs 11: 24 & 25; Luke 6: 38; Galatians 6: 9 & 10; Proverbs 29: 23; Matthew 7: 1-5; and many others that pertain to how we are supposed to act and what we are to avoid. In fact, it would be a good idea to review all of Proverbs. You might find something you have been ignoring.

As for me, let God judge whether or not I am lazy. Don't worry how others view me. And don't use yourself as the measuring stick by which you measure anyone, least of all...me. You cannot measure industriousness, ambition, and willingness to work in a right way by those means. Those standards are worldly and wrong.

They are how the world looks at and compares others. But we have been commanded to come out of the world, to put away the old and put on the new. We are not to be of this world though we are still living among its citizens. We are to be ambassadors of Heaven, having been called to be children of God. therefore, it is God's view of us, and His view alone, that matters.

We are called to love one another, to serve one another. Love does not judge. It does not condemn. It does not hold a grudge.

It does not provoke. It does not seek selfish gains. It does not heed gossip or hold opinions that lead to such. *It does not demand.*

It is unconditional. It is kind. It remains patient above and beyond expectation. It seeks to give peace, encouragement, and words of comfort. It is willing to bear with for as long as it takes.

It understands. And all this, it does through God. You cannot accept God and not accept your neighbor. It's just that simple. If you hold a grudge against one of your own, do you not also hold a grudge against God? If you judge your own, do you not also judge God? If you condemn one of your own, do you not also condemn God?

Is it not written that we are *all* created in his likeness? And are we not all called to be HIs children? Then why do we insist on being at odds with one another? Why do we impose impossible expectations on one another? Why do we fight over that which we do not know for certain?

Pedant/ Hypocrite (2004)

(actual definition)

pedant:

1. A person who makes an excessive or inappropriate show of learning. 2(a). A person who overemphasizes rules or minor details. 2(b). A person who is pedantic, dogmatic, and formal.

———————————

Hypocrite:

A PERSON WHO PRETENDS to have desirable or publicly approved attitudes, beliefs, principles, etc. they do not actually possess. (taken from the greek Hypokrites- stage actor, hence "one who pretends to be what he is not")

A thought on True Love (2017)

WHEN TRUE LOVE ENTERS the picture, scars are seen as strength, and imperfections make you perfect in the eyes of those who truly love you. But then, true love makes two into one and there is no such thing as man or woman, just one heart, one mind, one soul, and one body that just happens to have two halves. There is no 'yours' or 'mine', it is ours. there is no *I*, there is only *We*.

Love (2017)

WHEN YOU TRY TO DESCRIBE real love to those who have never experienced it, they cannot fathom what you are talking about. They only understand one of three worldly views of love. These worldly views are as follows:

1. Lust. This is *always* mistaken as love. The desire to have sexual contact with a woman (or man) simply because they are attractive and you feel that they are 'perfect' at that moment. There are no real connections here. And this, for the most part, is why so many marriages fail.

2. The desire to procreate. Like lust, this is a false pretense and usually ends badly for a couple.

3. The humanly perverted version of pure love, with conditions added. This is the concept most "Christians" think of when they hear the word 'love'. This is a perversion and is *not* love. It does not lead to two becoming one or both understanding each other on a soul-level. It only leads to bitterness and contempt when the illusions painted by both/either fade and they are left with the reality. There is always a selfish motive, often falsified as a "Godly" motive, attached to this. The recipient either has to "convert" to the other's way of thinking (as in religion), change their lifestyle, or be subservient or risk being punished by the other in a myriad of ways because of their refusal.

True love, real love, is an experience that runs soul-deep. It unites heart, mind, soul, and body as one and immerses the two halves that have united completely. It erases the need for master and servant because both halves are revealed to be equal, not superior or inferior. It strips away the need to control because the two think as one. It makes it impossible for any outside force to break the bond.

There is a peace that no emotion, no physical draw, no chemical temptation, or primal drive can ever deliver. With that peace comes a oneness with the universe (or with God, if you wish) that cannot be found anywhere else. Oneness with your mate is oneness with nature and the universe. You have a strength that cannot be found anywhere else.

You have something that very few really understand. And this lack of understanding tends to cause friction in the form of envy. This envy manifests itself as desperation, a need to belittle, or to contradict especially in times when the other partner stands up to defend their other half. Those who become envious do not understand the reality that *is* love. They only see that they can no longer bully those who are immersed in love.

Another thing that most do not understand is that those who are blessed enough to experience this kind of love can never truly love another should one or the other mate die. There is no replacement for it and the love itself does not die, even if a part of the mate left behind does. This is because a couple that shares this kind of love normally dies within months or years of each other...and often die together or within minutes or hours of each other. Rarely is a member of a union like this ever left behind. They cannot survive long without the other half.

Saying things like "you'll find another" or "you're young" are the wrong things to say to someone who has experienced this kind of love and had their other half die. One will never "find someone new" after a love like this. They cannot love as deeply. Nor do they ever desire to. They simply want to finish what they have been left to do so they can reunite with their other half as soon as possible.

Presidential Platform (2016/17)

PRESIDENTIAL PLATFORM: education

Abolition of Common core and a return to traditional educational styles with the exception of implementation of what is learned from studying educational systems abroad.

Transparency of current private charters for review of funds, where funds go, educational implementation of funding, annual salaries of executive and teaching staff, and actual success/failure report. Noncompliance will result in the closure of charter in question.

There is to be a moratorium set on new private charters and a cap set upon how much they receive from the federal government.

Our current public education will be preserved and the process through which funding is given shall be reviewed and reformed so that schools are properly funded despite number of students, area/region of schools, and main population of students (IE minority/majority).

A new Presidential reading/literacy program will be a key project, thus promoting literacy and reading. As literacy is key to every child's success, it is held in high regard and as reading is key to successfully navigating life, and negotiating contracts, it is of the utmost importance.

Arts and sciences will hold an important part in educational funding. Music and the arts are important for the advancement of science and math and are key to success in school. Without the arts, children do not meet or exceed their potential in school.

Higher education is key to success. All online for-profit colleges shall submit to review. Those who do not meet or exceed educational requirements will be given a chance to meet requirements. If requirements are still not met, they will be put on probation for 90 days. If within 90 days, they still do not meet requirements, their accreditation will be suspended.

For lower income applicants, higher education will be given at lower or no cost so that their future prospects will be more than doubled. This is not, however, a free education. It is simply an opportunity given through the responsibilities of both the educational system and the governments, both state and federal.

For rural pursuants of higher education, who opt to not go to campus learning due to work or entrepreneurial endeavors, will be able to take any course pertaining to their educational needs online from the school of their choice in the comfort of their own home.

Homeschooling parents will need to obtain, through a community college, a certification that shows that they have enough education to teach (a teaching certificate) and will be expected to take courses from time to time to stay updated on changes to education curriculum and standards.

There will be a bridge project between the Department of Education, the Department of Labor, and the Small Business Administration to promote young entrepreneurship This project will promote entrepreneurship among our youth and promote a competitive marketplace, thus creating a strong capitalist economy while removing the corporatist movement from economics.

Health and wellness also plays an important role in education. Exercise and good nutrition are integral to a strong mind and excellence in learning. Teaching proper nutrition and physical fitness should be a part of every school's curriculum will be insisted upon.

Proper education in women's health, as well as male health, shall be implemented into the current education.

The following shall be reimplemented into high school education: political science/civics, Social Studies (the study of cultures and peoples. This includes an overview of ALL religions, not just Christianity, that dissects and explores both the similarities and the differences of all so that students will know what is and is not acceptable among other cultures.), geography, in depth American and world history, as well as music (band and vocal) and art. Most, if not all, of these-along with 1-2 years of the foreign language of the student's choice (should be at least 3 choices per school) will be required for graduation. This is needed in order to compete in the world market and to succeed in business and to make it in the new global economy.

TAX PLATFORM

The rich have gotten away with paying a proportionally smaller tax than the majority of Americans. I propose lowering the taxes of the majority, those who make $100,000 or less, and raise the taxes of those who make $101,000 and above. This raise will be to a 90% rate with the ability to lower it significantly according to what they choose to do with their excess.

For instance, without being active in the community, those whose taxes raise to 90% , the rate will remain at 90%. This rate will drop only if those affected personally choose to go out into their communities and become active in charitable work within those areas that are economically disadvantaged. These options include working in a soup kitchen, homeless shelter, nonprofit medical facility, social advocacy facility, and/or volunteer services such as fire department or emergency medical services (EMT). Other options can also include working in the area of refugee relief services, Peace corps, doctors without borders, Unicef, or any volunteer conservation organization.

Corporate taxes will also rise to a 90% rate. Like the individual tax, this rate can be lowered according to whether the profits of the company are used for expansion, jobs creation, or equipment upgrades. Based off Eisenhower's original 90% tax plan, this tax is designed to cause jobs growth and to strengthen the economy. After all, money does not trickle down from the top, it flows up from the bottom.

Corporate taxes can and will be lowered for corporations if they create more jobs with money that would otherwise be sent as tax to the government, upgrade and keep corporate infrastructure up to date and state of the art, and expand business. It will also be lowered as long as corporations also use their profits to raise wages and salaries for their employees while keeping the top salaries at a point where profits are not lost through them.

Also: any business that has money overseas in "tax shelters" will be audited on a yearly basis and will be taxed according to what their offshore accounts contain. This means that hiding money in offshore accounts will be considered tax evasion and embezzling. A true accounting of all profits and their use will now be expected according to truth in business regulations, to be explained in another section.

<u>Economic reform</u>

Economically, America has had a tradition of being a capitalistic country. In recent years, at least the last 20-30, the economy has taken a decidedly frightening corporatist appearance, corporations taking command of writing-or unwriting-regulations. Corporatism is unhealthy and destructive. It thrives only on the supply side of the supply and demand scale and neglects to understand that supply should always be driven by genuine demand/need for a product or service. It incorrectly sees the consumer as less important than the bottom line and assumes that money "trickles down" from the top to those at the bottom. This view is incorrect and omits the importance of wages in the drive and demand for products. This corporatist tendency will come to an end and a healthy capitalistic free market will once again resume.

In a healthy capitalist economy, the market is freely competitive and is driven by the demand side of the supply and demand scale.

The healthy market is also marked by a certain level of government regulatory action to ensure that the market remains solvent. Thus supply, demand, income, and regulations create a delicate balance that creates an entrepreneurial spirit in all Americans and drives innovation. Without innovation, there is no advancement. Without advancement, there is stagnation. Where there is stagnation, there is infrastructure decay.

To aid the economy, we will turn our attention to the individual community and foster the desire for every community to expand their economies through encouraging individual entrepreneurship within the community. this shall be done through several incentives including education, government grants for both young and adult entrepreneurs, and through the fostering of inner community and intercommunity trade that will expand nationally.

With entrepreneurial incentives in place, the communities will be able to experience economic growth, helping state economies to grow, and eventually the national economy. Through this growth, we will be able to see a return of former economic strength and pride.

Corporate reform

As stated in the tax reform section, corporations will be made responsible for their own growth. Through the Eisenhower tax model, they will have to pay a 90% tax rate that they can lessen through growth, jobs creation, and proper distribution and usage of profits. This proper usage includes proper upkeep of the company, research and development of products, raising wages/salaries of their labor force, offering health/medical insurance for their labor force, and reinvestment into the business. The salaries of top management should not exceed a margin or 15-20% ($100,000-200,000/yr) above what they are willing to pay their labor force.

Also included is the expectation that every company will create more jobs through expansion. Expansion equals the purchase of new equipment, which equals more jobs. If a company decides that they cannot afford to follow this prescribed business path, they remain at 90%. Each prescribed action mentioned in the proper usage description will cut the corporate tax by 10%.

Monopolies will be dismantled and smaller companies (after all, smaller companies are easier to run and better able to create a profit) created. Diversity in the market will be restored and competition will resume.

Any company with more than 25% of their manufacturing outside the United States will be considered a foreign corporation and they will be asked to move their world headquarters out of the US, if they wish to remain, they will be requested to move at least 90% of their manufacturing back stateside. If they refuse, they will lose their citizenship and they will be forced to move, a tariff or import tax placed upon their goods.

There will be massive cuts in corporate subsidies. Any large corporation receiving subsidies will be audited and their subsidies discontinued. Any corporation that can spend billions to influence legislation can afford to run without subsidies and can afford a tax increase.

Subsidies will be reserved for small and mid-size businesses only. Small business, by definition, is any business that makes $900,000 or less. A mid-size business, by definition, is any business making $901,000 - $66,000,000 (est.) yearly(Merritt,2017). Any company that makes above the $33,000,000 limit will automatically be considered a large corporation and will be ineligible for subsidies or government funding.

Small/ mid-sized business reform

Taxes for small and midsized businesses will be less strict. As small and midsized businesses are focused more on growth than the bottom line, they tend to be the largest supplier of jobs, though the smaller businesses are severely limited in this area due to financial constraints. Incentives will be put in place to ensure that subsidies each business needs will be available as needed.

These subsidies will be available according to need. Those small and midsized businesses that need more will receive as their need dictates, those needing less will likewise receive according to need. Stricter regulations will be put into place to ensure that this is done as described and that no corporation making above the prescribed ceiling receives.

Subsidies are for the growth and stabilization of smaller businesses, not the greed of the larger corporations and it is time that these funds are placed where they belong. The gluttonous greed that has occurred in previous decades shall be halted and the prosperity this country has enjoyed in the past shall be brought back through the promotion and growth of new businesses and existing small businesses, while limiting the power of the corporations that have taken their status in this country for granted.

A part of this reform is the proposed creation of a program within the Small Business Administration that is twofold. The first part of this new program is educational, intended to teach young aspiring entrepreneurs how to properly run a business. The second, which is to take place while the young entrepreneur is learning proper business management, will be the funding of their choice of business. The program shall tentatively be called The Future Entrepreneur/Business Owner Incentive Program and shall be offered to all American youth who desire to open a business of their own. There is no tentative lower age limit for this program, the age cap being set at 18 (age when most youth head for college) though older youth may apply if they do not wish to go on to college, so it can even be used as a way to teach through such small business opportunities as the summer lemonade stand or baked goods table, anything that can possibly be used to teach a child how to run a business.

A similar incentive will be implemented for adults wishing to begin a business later in their life, between the ages of 35 and 75 (or older), to build their dream business and add to the local economies where they live. Like the youth program, it will be twofold and offer education as well as funding. The tentative name of this program will be the older adult entrepreneurial Incentive Program and will be open to all who fall within the age criteria.

For communities, we will create a program to promote the entrepreneurial and economic growth within the community and promote patronage of locally operated businesses. With community economic growth, the states will encounter economic growth and eventually the country as well. Only through focusing on individual communities first, building their businesses and economies, can we truly build this nation's economy and restore our markets to a healthy and strong position.

Religious tax exemption reform

This great country was built on diversity. There is nothing religious about the Constitution or any of the records that discuss how that Constitution was formed. Nor were the founding fathers truly accepting of, as they were recorded as saying, "that vile and cruel institution known as slavery". In the debates recorded in the *Antifederalist Papers*, they debated whether or not to abolish the institution while they brought together the ideas that would later become the Constitution but decided-for sake of Union and to prevent the newly formed southern states-to reluctantly allow it. Their original desire was to make *all* men free, not just the white Anglo-Saxon American.

Their ideal was to create a government where leadership was kept separate from religion, where all could live free. This separation of church and state was meant to preserve the Union and to prevent the bloodshed that Europe had seen over its history as a religion-driven mass of kingships and duchies. To ensure that this separation remains intact, the tax exemption of churches will be audited and any church engaged in political intrigue and policy making will lose those exemption privileges until such time that they amend their behavior and return to being a moral compass for their followers rather than the judges, juries, and executioners they have attempted to become of those they saw as morally deviant.

To remind our religious brethren of their place, I must remind them of Christ's command to love unconditionally. This means that there should be no boundaries. Their love should not rest upon whether a person is heterosexual, Christian, white, or identify as the gender they were born but rather without bounds and without expectations. Unconditional.

I must also remind our Christian brethren that hate, greed, and selfish expectations have no place in the Christian heart. Nor does the lust for power or the lust for another. Since Christ gave each and every Christian a choice, it is not the place of any to legislate away another person's choices. Nor is it the place of any Christian to force upon another the capitulation to their belief.

As a country based on freedom of religion (or freedom not to hold to religion), the United States will not abide the abuse of said freedom by any claiming that the right gives them a right to use their religion as a weapon of oppression. Remember your history: the first colonists left England to have the freedom to worship as they pleased. Though they soon forgot the oppression they fled from and oppressed others, their descendants-our forefathers, one generation removed from those who had committed atrocities in the name of religion-had learned and attempted to prevent any future reprisals of that horror through separating church and state and including the freedom of religion within the constitution.

Thus, any religious entity that violates the rights of another to worship (or refrain from worship) in the manner they choose will lose tax exemption and also be expected to amend their behavior according to the Constitution.

All mega churches will lose their exemption. Any institution that preys upon the poor and sells a product, whether it be shoes or the "word of God", is a business not a church. This very act of selling removes any exemption from tax. Like all corporations, these mega churches will have a 90% tax which can be lessened according to the work they do in their communities, their states, and within the country. Any foreign work will not be eligible to be used for this purpose, only domestic work.

The work that will be eligible to go toward the lowering of their tax load are as follows:

1. Delivering food and nonreligious services to the poor, needy, ill, handicapped, and elderly

2. community projects consisting of renovation of buildings. This includes the purchase of materials needed, help offered in the form of workers, meals for the builders, and the establishing of trust between the communities and themselves through restraint and lack of proselytizing.

3. random acts of kindness. Without conditions and without preaching to those you are being kind to. Remember, actions speak louder than words and often times, a kind deed has more impact than any number of words.

4. quit attacking public education. There is nothing wrong with the system, at least not in the manner you present it. You do not need more religious charters, you need to learn how to mingle and be a part of this country.

When you, as an organization, can quit trying to control those around you and realize that your belief is more a personal lifestyle than a political power, you will regain exemption.

Political reform

Both parties will submit to an independent investigation of party policies and methods of doing business. Those members taking money from lobbyists will be prosecuted for taking bribes and lobbyists will be prosecuted for bribery. Both will be charged with corruption and ethics violations. The rule dealing with lobbyist money and lobbyists in general will be amended to eject all lobbyists from legislative chambers and to make taking lobbyist money illegal as bribery.

The only lobbyists allowed in Washington DC will be those that lobby for veteran's rights and the needs of our veterans.

Any politician who believes in war, but does not believe in taking care of the veterans of those wars or the refugees those wars create will be removed from their office and replaced. Any politician who claims to be prolife but deems the poor, handicapped, elderly, widow, terminally ill, black, Hispanic, Muslim, Jew, Native American, orphaned or child to be less than worthy of their service shall be removed from office and replaced. You cannot be prolife without loving *all* life, no matter the color, creed, age, health, gender, gender identity, or sexual orientation.

As law makers, we are there to do what is in the best interest of our constituents, not just a minority who holds money. We are not there to change the rules and create a religious utopia for those who want to erase the reasons this country was founded.

Any politician who has ties to any hate group will be removed from office and replaced. Any politician who is revealed to be a sexual predator and is to be sentenced will be removed from office and struck from the record as if they have never served. Public service does not lessen the seriousness nor should it determine the sentence once convicted. There is no excuse for such actions and the perpetrator shall be expected to serve full sentence without leniency.

Any politician who wishes to make rights for rapists, or who wishes to make claims that rape does not exist is unfit for office as are those who claim that incest is perfectly fine. Within the context of every belief and philosophy, at least the major philosophies, these two moral wrongs have always been seen as cardinal sins. Any who condone such crimes are unfit to serve as lawmakers and should be investigated heavily. Any politician who calls for drug testing before receipt of government help shall themselves submit to a drug test before receiving their salary. Equal treatment for both representative and represented shall be observed.

ALEC, Citizens United, and all other corporate run organizations and political funding PACs will be disbanded as will the NRA. None of these organizations serve any useful purpose and only serve to undermine the rights of the average citizens.

Political mudslinging will cease. If we cannot stick to the issues and the platforms, neither candidate should be running. What is past is past, and bringing up the past-especially if your opponent has changed their views-is straying from the issues. No using nonissues. These nonissues include:

1. illegals taking away jobs. Currently, most jobs have been leaving the country, so they cannot be taken by anyone except people in the countries where those jobs are headed.

2. Islam being taught in public schools. Last public school I was in taught no such thing. Unless you have stepped foot in one of those Turkish run charter schools and mistook it as a "public" school, no public school teaches any religion. They might research or give an assignment to research and learn a little about a culture and their religion in Social Studies, but no one teaches religion in a public school.

3. fear of a minority or of refugees. Minorities are not a problem. Neither are refugees. As Roosevelt said, "we have nothing to fear except fear itself" (FDR, 1930).

4. loss of whiteness. First of all "racism" or ethnic hatred as it should be termed, is just plain wrong. We are, after all, one race—the human—and are made in a variety of colors, just like flowers in a field. Diversity is what creates beauty. No one is going to lose their color, and even if they did, why are we even worried about it?

5. foreign non-Christian radical terrorists. We have a bigger problem here, stateside called domestic "Christian" terrorists. They congregate under different names: neo-Nazi, nationalists, white supremacists, "militant Christians" , fundamentalists, and the KKK, just to name a few. These groups pose a far greater threat to this country and its founding principles than any outside enemy, real or imagined. As for the supposed "radicalized" foreign terrorists, our constant wars have created those in the last twenty

years. Stop thinking that they have any bearing on where this country is headed.

6. gun rights. If we were to implement the second amendment as it is written, every gun owner would be *expected* to serve in the military. Individual gun rights hinged upon the individual's willingness to serve the new nation, thus-if we were to use the original purpose of the amendment-so would any gun owner today. To add to this, no civilian should ever need or desire to own military grade weapons such as an AK47, M27, or any sniper rifle. The argument that certain countries allow gun ownership is a nonpoint, since many European countries expect their citizens to serve in their militaries once they reach 18, as do many Central and South American countries. We are the only country that does not have a compulsory military service regulation or law, making us the only country that does not expect our youth to serve the country as a member of our military. While there once existed a military draft, it was phased out over twenty years ago and military service became an individual choice, except in times of extreme need, which hasn't happened since Vietnam.

7. transgender restroom privileges. Why are we even having an issue with this? My husband has often stated, during the Congressional debates on this non issue, that he was more worried about the men who were standing at the urinal next to him staring at what he had than he ever was about a transgender. Molesters are not transgender, they are average looking men and women who seem unassuming and who wait for the most opportune time, like when you leave your son/daughter alone in a public restroom thinking they are safe because "everyone is male/female and they wouldn't do anything". This is not, in any way, an attempt to create paranoia

where your fellow men or women are concerned. This is merely an attempt to make a point about who is and is not a possible danger to a child.

8. Homosexuality. In the 1990s, a study was done on why homophobic people acted out violently toward homosexuals and/ or transgender people. The result were surprising. 90% of the homophobic people studied were revealed to be experiencing secret homosexual tendencies. The resulting internal battle between their sexual feelings and their rationale made them violent or made them oppressive toward homosexuals and transgenders. While other studies have doubtlessly been performed, probably with the same results, the point being made is that homosexuality is a non issue and should not be a topic for political discussions or debates.

As a nation, we have had privileges others have only dreamed about. Let us not take our privileges for granted. Let us not make issues out of non issues.

Taxes to be instituted

Corporate Taxes: 90%

We're going back to the Eisenhower model. It has the following deductions as incentives for growth and equality. The initial corporate (any business with $1 billion and above in business yearly)

1. 10% new equipment deduction for any NEW equipment bought over the fiscal year to create new jobs.

2. 10% growth deduction for any expansion of a business to add more jobs in other towns/regions in the country.

3. 10% growth deduction for jobs created internally, within the business, in attempts to lower unemployment locally.

4. 5% deduction for pay equality within the company

5. 5% deduction for reinvesting at least 80% of all profits back into the business (Top tier salaries do not count as reinvestment.)

6. 5% deduction for employee benefits fostering within the business (again, top tier benefits do not count.)

7. 5% deduction for community involvement efforts.

With items 4-7, management MUST show accurate proof of activities outlined as possible deductions. Though this is same as 1-3, which business owners/heads MUST show accurate and detailed proof, 4-7 are not growth related but rather shows of fiscal responsibility and rely on good ethics and a strong empathy and desire to care for employees.

Tax on the wealthy: 90%

Again, we look to the Eisenhower model for business but convert it to encourage the wealthy to become active in their communities and to compel them to help the economy grow.

1. 10% deduction for philanthropic work (investing in small businesses, donating money to the arts, sponsoring a less fortunate community member's schooling, helping all within a community succeed in some way, donating food/clothing/nonperishables to a

homeless shelter. Donating goods to a battered women's shelter/ veteran's home/orphanage, donating a portion of your yearly income to a public school/college, etc.)

2. 10% deduction for donating time and labor to community service.

3. 10% deduction for mentoring

4. 5% deduction for promoting community harmony

5. 5% deduction for reeducating through experiencing life in the shoes of another (must be documented and must last more than 1 year)

6. 5% deduction for rebuilding the community's infrastructure.

7. 5% deduction for showing outstanding leadership.

Small business taxes will be significantly lower. (small business makes less than $25 million yearly)

This tax will remain at the current 15-25% but will include the same incentives as the Corporate tax model so that the small business can grow and succeed through being able to expand and provide more work.

Midsize business tax will be comparatively equal to the small business tax with the same benefits. Midsize businesses are those businesses that make less than $1 billion but more than $25 million.

Income tax reform

Income tax should be no less than 10% and no more than 25% for those who make $100,000 or less and no less than 25% and no more than 30% for those who make from $101,000-$400,000. No one, not even Congress, is exempt from this and should be expected to pay according to their income should they desire to have quality schools, roads, fire departments, and other infrastructure. Those making $400,000 and above will be expected to pay the 90% tax expected from the wealthy. With success comes responsibility to your country and your community.

All loopholes currently present in the income tax system shall be closed and easement shall be left for those who are of the majority rather than the minority (the 99% rather than the top 1%). Businesses will not have the loopholes they traditionally used to ease their "burdens". Instead, they will be forced to be fiscally responsible and be a positive force in their communities.

Other miscellaneous taxes:

Since there is a growing interest in such things as "Biblical Law", to give Christians a taste of their desire, there shall be the following taxes "levied" temporarily:

1. a hate tax: this tax will be levied on those who preach hate as a "Christian" trait. This will be a 10% tax on all.

2. greed tax: this tax will be levied upon all who preach "Health, Wealth, and Happiness" as a "Christian" way of life. This will be a 10% tax levied on any preacher or religious group caught teaching that greed is Biblically OK.

3. Rape/incest culture tax. This will be a 10% tax levied upon all who preach that rape or incest is OK and is a "Christian" trait.

4. A war tax: This will be a 10% tax levied upon all who preach war upon any culture, color, or country.

5. an oppression tax. This will be a 10% tax levied upon any who think that their religious convictions gives them license to oppress those who are not the same as them or who do not believe what they believe.

6. a "bully" tax. A 10 % tax on all who wish to be bullies.

7. selfishness tax. 10% for believing that God wants you to take everything away from the poor, handicapped, ill, or elderly. Remember: he who stops up his ears to the cry of the poor will also one day cry and not be heard; he who oppresses the needy mocks his maker. (Prov.)

Finally: any church or religious organization that has preached hate, oppression, intolerance, or has been politically active will hereby LOSE their tax exemption. Since you are in the business of selling the "Word of God", you will hereby be expected to pay taxes like any other business. Those that have used their tax exemption as a means to push their political agendas will find themselves heavily fined and expected to pay 20-50 years of back taxes. If they cannot, they will be expected to close their doors and cease all operations in the US.

Religious leaders have a responsibility to preach the word of Christ while also living according to the humility and lowness that Christ instructed you to live. Nowhere are Christians promised a bed of roses or power over the nations, and greed, hate, and fear are all anti-Christian belief systems. Love, Christians, is the underlying message of Christ's ministry. The writings of the Apostles were meant solely for those who believed. They were never meant for you to use as weapons. Acceptance and mercy without judgment or condemnation were supposed to be your hallmarks. One's station in life, one's personal weaknesses, one's personal life, and the color of one's skin was never subject for your approval.

Corporations: If you have the money to give your CEOs a raise every year and if you have enough money to influence politics, you have enough money to pay your employees livable wages and to create jobs. Your responsibility is not to stuff your pockets with your profits, your responsibility is to keep your companies fiscally solvent as well as your employees well-paid. You also have a responsibility to your communities, states, and nation to be leaders, not greedy savages.

Any corporation with more than 25% of its manufacturing outside of the country, or that is an international conglomerate, will be subject to having US citizenships revoked and a foreign tax/tariff imposed upon their goods. This tax/tariff will be dependent upon what percentage of your business is elsewhere. 26-29% will gain 26-29% tax/tariff, and anything over will gain whatever the percentage is in tax/tariffs.

Oil and coal companies:

Your taxes will remain at 99% while you refuse to seek alternative energy options to revert to, slowly phasing out your current source of income to help save this planet while we can, and to ease strain on the ever-diminishing oil and coal reserves. Until you come to the realization that we need to move on beyond fossil fuels, your taxation will remain high so that your profits can help combat the pollution and the negative environmental changes your industry has caused.

Platform on women's rights:

All are equal and have equal rights. It is by the grace of a mother that we are all born. Nine months, they carry us in the womb. Eighteen years, they raise us the best they can no matter whether we are male or female. It is by the love of a mother that we are shielded from most that would harm us; it is our mothers who teach us the most in our youth.

It is a woman's natural right to choose what is done to her body. Just as the rest of us are given a freedom of choice to do either right or wrong, so it is with women. As the equal to men, they are entitled to equal pay, equal rights, and equal status in our society.

Equal rights:

Any self-respecting man or woman also respects their mother. Out of respect, all should see women as their equal. Equal rights means that they stand on equal footing. Rational men see women not as stepping stones or slaves, to be submissive or subjugated, but as equals who are half of what it takes to create the perfect union, the perfect team. Only bullies and insecure men see things otherwise.

Ignorance sees women as weaker and yet it is the woman who bears the weight of the child for nine months and the pain of giving birth, not the man. It is the woman who cares for the sick child and puts up with her sick mate.

She has earned her right to vote. She has earned her right to have equal pay. She has even earned her right to have a choice where her body is concerned. She has even earned a right to stand among her male peers.

Let us establish the following:

1. pro-choice does *not*, by any means, mean pro-abortion. It simply means that a woman has the choice to make any decision that needs to be made where her body is concerned-whether that is aborting a pregnancy or preserving that life.

2. abortion is not just inclusive to the action of taking an unborn life, but also includes certain other procedures that are known under other names such as the D&C, among others. Abortion is not always an unnecessary procedure, nor are the majority always a choice made by the woman. It is a known fact that a majority of abortions are:

a. the product of the demands of a male who does not want a child and sees his woman as subservient

b. Medical reasons do trump personal desires and, thus, the advice of the doctor must at all times be taken into consideration.

c. Some medical procedures, such as D&Cs, are also listed as "Abortion" even though they are not. A stillbirth and miscarriages are also listed as abortions. Any law dictating "abortion rights" is a misnomer simply because "pro-life" advocates fail to understand the scope of the term and, therefore, seek selfishly to dictate to others what they deem acceptable.

Gun Rights:

As per the Constitution, we the people must fully read the "Right" to bear arms correctly and not just as an "Advocacy" group leads us to read it. We do have the right to bear arms, but only if we are willing to serve our country. " A well regulated Militia, being necessary to the security of a free State, the right of the people to keep and bear Arms, shall not be infringed." The reason for this "right" is made plain. We are to share a responsibility to the protection of this country if we desire the freedom to own arms. These arms do NOT include military grade weapons. We are not at war with ourselves, thus we do not need these weapons on the streets. Nor do we need open or concealed carry, since we are not a third world country or living in the Wild West.

Thus, laws concerning guns will be examined, struck down if unnecessary to the freedom we share, or strengthened if the need is apparent. Restrictions will be placed on those weapons that are not made for hunting or basic self-defense, and removed from any basic armament for everyday life. No guns will be confiscated from law abiding citizens, but will be removed from those who have been convicted of violent offenses committed with guns. Sensible gun reform will be discussed at length. Any organization that impedes the advance of reform will lose tax exemption upon first offense and will be disbanded upon third offense. All organizations must drop all profitable advertising and subsist solely on the membership dues coming from their members. If an organization cannot do this, then they shall disband. NO organization should be used as a front for weapons manufacturers as a means of adding profits to their sales. Any organization found to be acting as such will be temporarily disbanded and not allowed re-incorporation for at least three years.

The time of the lobbyist is over. Now we work for a government of the people, by the people, and for the people. Not a government for the corporation, of the corporation, or by the corporation.

Views on The Federalist/Anti-Federalist Papers

I BELIEVE THAT IT IS the duty of all Americans to read the Federalist and Anti-federalist Papers. Everything you think you know about US history is suddenly called into question by a handful of documents that range from States' rights, term limits, structure of government, compensation of representatives and how representation should be elected by the masses or by the states to whether or not to tax slave importation or to do away with slavery altogether.

All these things were being discussed by our founding fathers before the creation and ratification of the Constitution, 74 years before the Civil War. They talked about abolishing the institution of slavery before it became one of the reasons the States went to war against themselves. Their reason for not doing so? They hoped that the southern states would abolish it on their own accord. The omission of anything to do with slavery was a decision made so that the southern states would unite as part of the new country.

Our founding fathers wanted unity, not division. They were trying to give us a better country through setting the precedent to give decision to the states. yes, the debate was a long almost 2-year endeavor but they made a constitution that was a balance of points made by both federalist and anti-federalist alike. Though delicate, it is an excellent balance of both views that made a compromise to accommodate both ideals while attempting to establish a strong government with an equal balance.

A Revelation About Churches

CHURCHES SELL RELIGION. Religion is not enlightenment. It is the opposite. They have lost the basis of what they claim to believe and sell the customer on the physicalities, not the spiritual. They no longer care about the soul-or should I say, their own souls-preferring to "save" the soul of some hapless "sinner" while they commit the biggest sin of all in judging another. They continually crucify their "savior" in attempts to "purify" others, thus negating the original sacrifice. In essence, they are not what they claim to be, becoming the very anti-Christ they fear while claiming other religions are the anti-Christ. Their leaders become the very beast that they claim another to be.

<u>Life as an Alpha One Carrier</u>

Living as a carrier of Alpha 1 Antitrypsin deficiency has changed my life. While I am not suffering from it outwardly, I have to be careful what I do, where I work, and what environments I enter. I learned I carried the recessive gene for A-1-A (or AATD) when I was 35. I learned that the world, the jobs, I had known had just come to an end.

What is A-1-A? think of getting pneumonia and never being able to get rid of it. This is a warning sign, one of the symptoms they use to diagnose the genetic deficiency where A-1-A (Alpha 1 Antitrypsin protease) is either not being produced in a large enough quantity to heal damage done to the lungs or is not produced at all. In mild cases, A-1-A deficiency is barely noticeable (like in my case) and one can live a pretty normal life—except the part of having to cut your list of viable jobs down to almost nothing except office work of writing—aside from finding it harder to find work or health insurance.

<u>Emails From a Revolutionary</u>

Dear Sirs

I am no millionaire, but I have a proposal. As a member of the middle/lower class, I have witnessed first hand the devastation of a tax scam such as is currently being proposed. I would love to meet and explain my ideas to someone who would be willing to take a chance. The problem is that I do not know exactly who I need to contact and another problem is that I am running out of time. My ideas could have a lasting impact on political and the country for a very long time. They will also affect the economy in a positive manner.

Please feel free to call me at 1-712-374-2387. I would be more than willing to set up a time to meet and run through the ideas with you. My only request is that we meet as a group, not just a single representative (one-on-oone). in other words, I want to meet you all in the same way an entrepreneur would meet with potential investors.

I will admit that there are numerous potential risks and that these ideas may not gain much in the way of financial dividends, but they will yield great rewards when they serve their purpose.

Cordially

Jason O'Hara

note: I am trying to realize a few projects that my late wife and I felt would do this country great good. I am not seeking wealth or profit, just justice and a leveling of the playing filed for those who cannot afford to buy their representation.

─────────────

SIRS/ MA'AMS:

While I understand your reticence at working with a non-wealthy American, I must remind you (and all who seek change) revolution cannot happen, nor can change, without action. Just making videos and giving voice to an objection is not enough. I am willing to offer you my abilities as both a businessman and as a devoted American to help you begin the bloodless revolution that could very well set this country back on course. All you have to do is contact me.

As I stated in my last email, I am working on limited time. I am in ill health, and cannot work as if I have all the time in the world. I do have a plan, one which will only keep me visible, but will allow whoever desires to be a part of this project to be as involved as they see fit. While I can only offer to donate my time and energy, as well as my intellect, I know that together we can set America back on the right track.

Until recently, I was a Business management student. I made top marks in ethics, HR, business law, and macroeconomics. I would have made top marks in marketing and Microeconomics if I had not had several events come together at the same point in time and create a problem for me. I was also instrumental in helping my late wife get straight "A's" in political Science. I have an amazing grasp of the Constitution and the meaning of each amendment.

I also have a deep understanding of history. American, European, and ancient. I am a philosopher who observes life and trends. Moreover, I am a visionary with a desire to change history as it is being made. And, yes, I come from a long line of deeply rebellious and highly notable names in history.

While I may not be your typical ally, I am offering you my assistance in defeating the dangerous legislative and executive body that has surfaced recently. please call me at 1-712-374-2387. I would love to set up a time to meet and discuss this subject further. I have nothing to lose but my life, and in the immortal words of Nathan Hale, "I regret that I have but one life to lose for my country"...and I have often heard it said that the most dangerous person in the world is someone who has nothing left to lose.

The time for words is over. Now is the time for action, whether behind the scenes or out in the open. Let's be the beginning of the change that we seek, not just the weak voices of reason that fail to reach the ears of those too foolish to listen.

Cordially

Jason O'Hara

––––––––––––––

DEAR SIRS

I know that you are probably getting tired of my emails. So, let me introduce myself

I am Jason O'Hara. I write under the nom de plume Jaysen True Blood and I *am* a published author whose works are readily available on Amazon. I am also a little known Vocalist who has a single song on the market...even though it languishes unnoticed. You might say that I am a struggling entrepreneur who wants the same thing as you: to destroy this stupid tax cut that Congress has just passed.

The only difference between you and I is that I am at the opposite end of the wealth spectrum as you. In other words, I am an impoverished entrepreneur who is looking at losing the only hope I had of making a go in the world. I know that I probably won't even get noticed since I am neither rich nor powerful, but at least I try to get people's attention.

Everything I have written to you in my past emails is true. I would love to see organizations like yours go from simply making videos to actually doing something to make a difference. By ignoring those who may not be as fortunate as you, but might actually be able to help you in your endeavor, You may actually be ignoring something that just might enable people like you to effect change not yet imagined.

You see, I was born to a lower middle class family that saw themselves remaining as lower middle class even though the reality of their status was closer to being impoverished than actually being successful. I watched as my father wore himself out working for a company that promised to remain in the area "forever" only to be swindled out of his hard-earned pension/retirement when he was forced to retire early and take disability. I watched him battle cancer caused by the chemicals he was exposed to, put through medical review every year by the company which was trying to get out of paying him the disability he had earned. I also watched him die of the side effects of the cancer treatment ("dead" Tuberculosis), a pulmonary embolism.

I have also watched as the company he worked for moved out of the area, breaking their promise to be a "forever" job. Of course, I had seen the day approaching when they began hiring through temp services, effectively removing all full time positions. I have also watched as other jobs moved out of my area, never to return. Yes, I have witnessed what greed does firsthand. I have *lived* through it.

You and I are on the same level, philosophically. Our desire is the same thing. To make things right for the average citizen. The only difference is that I *am* an average citizen. I live the struggle everyday. In every way. Of course, there is also the fact that I can see that the day of getting points across through cute little protest videos are over. Now is a time when action is needed. Now is time to take this revolution to the next level. (no, I don't mean with guns and bullets, I mean through a complete shift of paradigms and views.)

Please call me. I would love to meet with you all and talk.

Cordially

Jason O'Hara

tel.: 1-712-374-2387

Home address: 1209 Filmore; Sidney, Iowa.

Mailing address: P.O. Box 14; Sidney, Iowa 51652

—————————————

SIRS/MADAMS:

Apparently, you would much rather run around and waste time making videos than actually doing something substantial. People, especially Republicans, do not care about the business practices of McDonald's. Hell. You can't even tell them that fast food may be fast, but it also puts you in your grave fast too. You can't convince the willfully ignorant that it is ignorant or that it has been duped by those who would rather see them dead.

Before you can re-educate, you must first disconnect them from the sources of misinformation and lies. You must first shut down the sources of the problem. THIS is the revolution I am talking about: shutting down the propaganda that misleads and misdirects. Shutting down the money machines that fund these sources of misinformation.

America has been divided, and is ready to be conquered. Not because I say so, but because it IS so. Our political system has seen to this by allowing Corporations into the legislative process, letting the banks write banking legislation, and communications corporations to buy away net neutrality.

Let me ask you a question:

Would you rather add to the propaganda problem? Or do you really want to make changes? Change cannot be made if we just make propaganda, no matter how true it may be. More propo only adds to the information overload.

If you continue to make propaganda (even though you are making edu-prop), you will continue to the Americans that would otherwise unite with you that you do not really desire change, but only want to make a half-hearted objection to something you brought to America's attention (although the poor among the opposition is fully convinced that they will get a sizable tax cut as well, even though it has been proven otherwise) as unnecessary and unwanted. I know that I write harsh words, but I do not have much time left. And all we are promised is today. Tomorrow may never come, and yesterday is already gone. But with my waning health, I am looking at quite a few less todays.

I know that the rich rarely cavort with "the less fortunate" or those who promote a revolution in mind, thought, and ways of life. We tend to be a threat to you because of how we think. You fear visionaries, revolutionaries, and pioneers. You shun trailblazers.

But there is a time and a place for all things. Now is the time to lay aside class divisions and to work together with those you "feel obligated to protect" in order to shift paradigms and views. Now is the time for you to step out from behind your propo cameras and unite with the majority of America in an effort to take back this country from a handful of your own and return it to the control of the majority once more.

─────────

OR ARE YOU AFRAID?

─────────

CORDIALLY

Jason O'Hara

Tel.: 1-712-374-2387

(5 AM-9:30 AM CST; 11 AM-8 PM CST)

physical address: 1209 Filmore; Sidney, Iowa (45 minutes south of Omaha, 6 hrs west/Southwest of Des Moines, 5-6 hours north of KC)

P.O. Box 14; Sidney, Iowa 51652

─────────

PS...I HAVE 1-2 WEEKS before I need to be somewhere else, hence the urgency. Am trying to get things set up before that time. Please. answer me.

———————————

FROM THE DESK OF JASON L. O'Hara

1209 Filmore

P.O. Box 14

Sidney, Iowa 51652

1-712-374-2387

To: Patriotic Millionaires

———————————

DEAR SIRS:

Please forgive me for saying that, for the most part, you are preaching to the choir with your videos. Sadly, the main body of the Republican Party does not believe the truth anymore because they have been misinformed, misled, and miseducated. Only by unplugging the sources of the misinformation can we truly achieve the first major step of change. The only way to unplug these sources of misinformation is to make their financial sources dry up. To do this, we will need help.

I want to offer you my help, but I also need your help. I do not want anything from you except connections. The type of connections that can help me achieve the objective I have mentioned. The result will be a win for all, not just a small group. I have already said that I will work for free, as a volunteer. I have also offered to be the only visible face of this endeavor.

I have called this a Revolution. In every way, it is. But it does not include a war or any violence. It is more a revolution in thought and paradigms. A change from old ways to new. I do not have time to mess with people who would rather make half-hearted gestures to their less fortunate countrymen, I want people with guts. Stamina. The willingness to fight alongside your fellow Americans for what is right, rather than running around irresponsibly wasting time and effort on videos that are received with deaf ears and dead hearts. You cannot change their willful ignorance without first shutting down what keeps them that way.

I want to join forces with you. I want to help you take your organization to the next level. And I can. I excelled in ethics, Business law, economics, and Human Resources when I was still in classes (I had to leave due to financial hardship and have not been able to return). I also have a mind for politics and Constitutional law. By the way, I do plan on going back to school as soon as I can get back on my feet.

Ironically, the plan I have is simple, but I would much rather discuss such a thing in person. As I have nothing to win, nothing to lose, and nothing to prove....the next move is yours.

I am sending you some links to my blogs. Clues to who I am and how I think are there. I am also sending you the link to my books, so you can see that I am, indeed, an author and that I am willing to be open with you.

https://darkfantasyindependentmoviereviews.wordpress.com[1]

https://darkportalreviews.wordpress.com[2]

https://theradiopiratepresents.wordpress.com[3]

https://jaysworldcomix.wordpress.com[4]

https://jaysentrueblood.wordpress.com[5]

https://jayspoetryjournal.wordpress.com[6]

https://theadventuresandstoriesofhh.wordpress.com[7]

https://themusicandlyricsofjaytruebllood.wordpress.com/

https://thenonfictionandarticlesofjaytrueblood.wordpress.com[8]

http://www.amazon.com/Jaysen-True-Blood/e/B00IUNJWFI/

I write under the pseudonym Jaysen True Blood. I am also a vocalist and avid student of life. Unfortunately, I am saddened by the current events.

I also know my time grows short. that is why I am willing to work with you on this endeavor. Please. Give this some serious thought.

---

1. https://darkfantasyindependentmoviereviews.wordpress.com/

2. https://darkportalreviews.wordpress.com/

3. https://theradiopiratepresents.wordpress.com/

4. https://jaysworldcomix.wordpress.com/

5. https://jaysentrueblood.wordpress.com/

6. https://jayspoetryjournal.wordpress.com/

7. https://theadventuresandstoriesofhh.wordpress.com/

8. https://thenonfictionandarticlesofjaytrueblood.wordpress.com/

Come out of your comfort zone and join your brothers and sisters in trying to do something rather than just making noise .

─────────

CORDIALLY

Jason O'Hara

─────────

FROM THE DESK OF JASON L. O'Hara

1209 Filmore

P.O. Box 14

Sidney, Iowa 51652

tel.: 1-712-374-2387

Sirs

Those who sit on their asses and do nothing are just as bad as those who do despicable deeds. When you are outraged about a policy, but only make videos, that makes you just as bad as those who literally WROTE the policy. Being proactive is what I do best. I am a nuisance to those who want me to go away. I am determined to make change THROUGH ACTION, not through simply making videos or saying that something is an outrage.

I have literally written a political platform. I wrote it for my late wife because she was going to run for President in 2020. I was also going to run, but I am not sure that I have enough time left to do so. I gave you the links to my books and my blogs so that you could familiarize yourself with who I am and what I think.

I am greatly saddened that you have proven to be less interested in doing something substantial, something active. It saddens me that you believe that you can change the world one video at a time, without following up with action. Real action. But, then, maybe you are just like the rest of the rich: only willing to put out minimal effort while still saving face with your peers. Perhaps you aren't as opposed to the tax scam as you claim, but want the poorer Americans to believe your swill.

I am not judging you, but this is how it looks to the masses. I know, because I am down here with the others starving. If hunger is what is needed, I am hungry. But I am NOT greedy. Greed solves nothing. A ho-hum attitude or half-assed attempt gains nothing either. Either you are fully invested, or you are simply trying to make people love you. If you are fully invested, you will eagerly want to know more about my ideas. Otherwise, America is truly lost.

Let me leave you with this:

The only way to teach humility is to remove the source of ones pride. We have a small segment of population who are overly proud of being wealthy. It is time they have been taught humility. They wrote a bill to destroy America. It is time to bring them to ruin before they ruin this beautiful country.

———————————

CORDIALLY

Jason O'Hara

Note: the only way to get me to quit emailing is to set up a meeting.

———————————

FROM THE DESK OF JASON L. O'Hara

1209 Filmore

P.O. Box 14

Sidney Iowa 51652

Tel.: 1-712-374-2387

Sirs

Below is the Presidential Platform (rough form) I wrote for my late wife. I was going to be a part of her 2020 presidential campaign team. Perhaps, if you saw exactly what I can do, and how I think, you might find me a great asset.

———————————

Presidential Platform (2016/17)

PRESIDENTIAL PLATFORM: education

Abolition of Common core and a return to traditional educational styles with the exception of implementation of what is learned from studying educational systems abroad.

Transparency of current private charters for review of funds, where funds go, educational implementation of funding, annual salaries of executive and teaching staff, and actual success/failure report. Noncompliance will result in the closure of charter in question.

There is to be a moratorium set on new private charters and a cap set upon how much they receive from the federal government.

Our current public education will be preserved and the process through which funding is given shall be reviewed and reformed so that schools are properly funded despite number of students, area/region of schools, and main population of students (IE minority/majority).

A new Presidential reading/literacy program will be a key project, thus promoting literacy and reading. As literacy is key to every child's success, it is held in high regard and as reading is key to successfully navigating life, and negotiating contracts, it is of the utmost importance.

Arts and sciences will hold an important part in educational funding. Music and the arts are important for the advancement of science and math and are key to success in school. Without the arts, children do not meet or exceed their potential in school.

Higher education is key to success. All online for-profit colleges shall submit to review. Those who do not meet or exceed educational requirements will be given a chance to meet requirements. If requirements are still not met, they will be put on probation for 90 days. If within 90 days, they still do not meet requirements, their accreditation will be suspended.

For lower income applicants, higher education will be given at lower or no cost so that their future prospects will be more than doubled. This is not, however, a free education. It is simply an opportunity given through the responsibilities of both the educational system and the governments, both state and federal.

For rural pursuants of higher education, who opt to not go to campus learning due to work or entrepreneurial endeavors, will be able to take any course pertaining to their educational needs online from the school of their choice in the comfort of their own home.

Homeschooling parents will need to obtain, through a community college, a certification that shows that they have enough education to teach (a teaching certificate) and will be expected to take courses from time to time to stay updated on changes to education curriculum and standards.

There will be a bridge project between the Department of Education, the Department of Labor, and the Small Business Administration to promote young entrepreneurship This project will promote entrepreneurship among our youth and promote a competitive marketplace, thus creating a strong capitalist economy while removing the corporatist movement from economics.

Health and wellness also plays an important role in education. Exercise and good nutrition are integral to a strong mind and excellence in learning. Teaching proper nutrition and physical fitness should be a part of every school's curriculum will be insisted upon.

Proper education in women's health, as well as male health, shall be implemented into the current education.

The following shall be reimplemented into high school education: political science/civics, Social Studies (the study of cultures and peoples. This includes an overview of ALL religions, not just

Christianity, that dissects and explores both the similarities and the differences of all so that students will know what is and is not acceptable among other cultures.), geography, in depth American and world history, as well as music (band and vocal) and art. Most, if not all, of these-along with 1-2 years of the foreign language of the student's choice (should be at least 3 choices per school) will be required for graduation. This is needed in order to compete in the world market and to succeed in business and to make it in the new global economy.

TAX PLATFORM

The rich have gotten away with paying a proportionally smaller tax than the majority of Americans. I propose lowering the taxes of the majority, those who make $100,000 or less, and raise the taxes of those who make $101,000 and above. This raise will be to a 90% rate with the ability to lower it significantly according to what they choose to do with their excess.

For instance, without being active in the community, those whose taxes raise to 90% , the rate will remain at 90%. This rate will drop only if those affected personally choose to go out into their communities and become active in charitable work within those areas that are economically disadvantaged. These options include working in a soup kitchen, homeless shelter, nonprofit medical facility, social advocacy facility, and/or volunteer services such as fire department or emergency medical services (EMT). Other options can also include working in the area of refugee relief services, Peace corps, doctors without borders, Unicef, or any volunteer conservation organization.

Corporate taxes will also rise to a 90% rate. Like the individual tax, this rate can be lowered according to whether the profits of the company are used for expansion, jobs creation, or equipment upgrades. Based off Eisenhower's original 90% tax plan, this tax is designed to cause jobs growth and to strengthen the economy. After all, money does not trickle down from the top, it flows up from the bottom.

Corporate taxes can and will be lowered for corporations if they create more jobs with money that would otherwise be sent as tax to the government, upgrade and keep corporate infrastructure up to date and state of the art, and expand business. It will also be lowered as long as corporations also use their profits to raise wages and salaries for their employees while keeping the top salaries at a point where profits are not lost through them.

Also: any business that has money overseas in "tax shelters" will be audited on a yearly basis and will be taxed according to what their offshore accounts contain. This means that hiding money in offshore accounts will be considered tax evasion and embezzling. A true accounting of all profits and their use will now be expected according to truth in business regulations, to be explained in another section.

Economic reform

Economically, America has had a tradition of being a capitalistic country. In recent years, at least the last 20-30, the economy has taken a decidedly frightening corporatist appearance, corporations taking command of writing-or unwriting-regulations. Corporatism is unhealthy and destructive. It thrives only on the supply side of the supply and demand scale and neglects to understand that supply should always be driven by genuine demand/need for a product or service. It incorrectly sees the consumer as less important than the bottom line and assumes that money "trickles down" from the top to those at the bottom. This view is incorrect and omits the importance of wages in the drive and demand for products. This corporatist tendency will come to an end and a healthy capitalistic free market will once again resume.

In a healthy capitalist economy, the market is freely competitive and is driven by the demand side of the supply and demand scale. The healthy market is also marked by a certain level of government regulatory action to ensure that the market remains solvent. Thus supply, demand, income, and regulations create a delicate balance that creates an entrepreneurial spirit in all Americans and drives innovation. Without innovation, there is no advancement. Without advancement, there is stagnation. Where there is stagnation, there is infrastructure decay.

To aid the economy, we will turn our attention to the individual community and foster the desire for every community to expand their economies through encouraging individual entrepreneurship within the community. this shall be done through several incentives including education, government grants for both young and adult entrepreneurs, and through the fostering of inner community and intercommunity trade that will expand nationally.

With entrepreneurial incentives in place, the communities will be able to experience economic growth, helping state economies to grow, and eventually the national economy. Through this growth, we will be able to see a return of former economic strength and pride.

Corporate reform

As stated in the tax reform section, corporations will be made responsible for their own growth. Through the Eisenhower tax model, they will have to pay a 90% tax rate that they can lessen through growth, jobs creation, and proper distribution and usage of profits. This proper usage includes proper upkeep of the company, research and development of products, raising wages/salaries of their labor force, offering health/medical insurance for their labor force, and reinvestment into the business. The salaries of top management should not exceed a margin or 15-20% ($100,000-200,000/yr) above what they are willing to pay their labor force.

Also included is the expectation that every company will create more jobs through expansion. Expansion equals the purchase of new equipment, which equals more jobs. If a company decides that they cannot afford to follow this prescribed business path, they remain at 90%. Each prescribed action mentioned in the proper usage description will cut the corporate tax by 10%.

Monopolies will be dismantled and smaller companies (after all, smaller companies are easier to run and better able to create a profit) created. Diversity in the market will be restored and competition will resume.

Any company with more than 25% of their manufacturing outside the United States will be considered a foreign corporation and they will be asked to move their world headquarters out of the US, if they wish to remain, they will be requested to move at least 90% of their manufacturing back stateside. If they refuse, they will lose their citizenship and they will be forced to move, a tariff or import tax placed upon their goods.

There will be massive cuts in corporate subsidies. Any large corporation receiving subsidies will be audited and their subsidies discontinued. Any corporation that can spend billions to influence legislation can afford to run without subsidies and can afford a tax increase.

Subsidies will be reserved for small and mid-size businesses only. Small business, by definition, is any business that makes $900,000 or less. A mid-size business, by definition, is any business making $901,000 - $66,000,000 (est.) yearly(Merritt,2017). Any company that makes above the $33,000,000 limit will automatically be considered a large corporation and will be ineligible for subsidies or government funding.

Small/ mid-sized business reform

Taxes for small and midsized businesses will be less strict. As small and midsized businesses are focused more on growth than the bottom line, they tend to be the largest supplier of jobs, though the smaller businesses are severely limited in this area due to financial constraints. Incentives will be put in place to ensure that subsidies each business needs will be available as needed.

These subsidies will be available according to need. Those small and midsized businesses that need more will receive as their need dictates, those needing less will likewise receive according to need. Stricter regulations will be put into place to ensure that this is done as described and that no corporation making above the prescribed ceiling receives.

Subsidies are for the growth and stabilization of smaller businesses, not the greed of the larger corporations and it is time that these funds are placed where they belong. The gluttonous greed that has occurred in previous decades shall be halted and the prosperity this country has enjoyed in the past shall be brought back through the promotion and growth of new businesses and existing small businesses, while limiting the power of the corporations that have taken their status in this country for granted.

A part of this reform is the proposed creation of a program within the Small Business Administration that is twofold. The first part of this new program is educational, intended to teach young aspiring entrepreneurs how to properly run a business. The second, which is to take place while the young entrepreneur is learning proper business management, will be the funding of their choice of business. The program shall tentatively be called The Future Entrepreneur/Business Owner Incentive Program and shall be offered to all American youth who desire to open a business of their own. There is no tentative lower age limit for this program, the age cap being set at 18 (age when most youth head for college) though older youth may apply if they do not wish to go on to college, so it can even be used as a way to teach through such small business opportunities as the summer lemonade stand or baked goods table, anything that can possibly be used to teach a child how to run a business.

A similar incentive will be implemented for adults wishing to begin a business later in their life, between the ages of 35 and 75 (or older), to build their dream business and add to the local economies where they live. Like the youth program, it will be twofold and offer education as well as funding. The tentative name of this program will be the older adult entrepreneurial Incentive Program and will be open to all who fall within the age criteria.

For communities, we will create a program to promote the entrepreneurial and economic growth within the community and promote patronage of locally operated businesses. With community economic growth, the states will encounter economic growth and eventually the country as well. Only through focusing on individual communities first, building their businesses and economies, can we truly build this nation's economy and restore our markets to a healthy and strong position.

Religious tax exemption reform

This great country was built on diversity. There is nothing religious about the Constitution or any of the records that discuss how that Constitution was formed. Nor were the founding fathers truly accepting of, as they were recorded as saying, "that vile and cruel institution known as slavery". In the debates recorded in the *Antifederalist Papers*, they debated whether or not to abolish the institution while they brought together the ideas that would later become the Constitution but decided-for sake of Union and to prevent the newly formed southern states-to reluctantly allow it. Their original desire was to make all men free, not just the white Anglo-Saxon American.

Their ideal was to create a government where leadership was kept separate from religion, where all could live free. This separation of church and state was meant to preserve the Union and to prevent the bloodshed that Europe had seen over its history as a religion-driven mass of kingships and duchies. To ensure that this separation remains intact, the tax exemption of churches will be audited and any church engaged in political intrigue and policy making will lose those exemption privileges until such time that they amend their behavior *and return to being a moral compass for their followers rather than the judges, juries, and executioners they have attempted to become of those they saw as morally deviant.*

To remind our religious brethren of their place, I must remind them of Christ's command to love unconditionally. This means that there should be no boundaries. Their love should not rest upon whether a person is heterosexual, Christian, white, or identify as the gender they were born but rather without bounds and without expectations. Unconditional.

I must also remind our Christian brethren that hate, greed, and selfish expectations have no place in the Christian heart. Nor does the lust for power or the lust for another. Since Christ gave each and every Christian a choice, it is not the place of any to legislate away another person's choices. Nor is it the place of any Christian to force upon another the capitulation to their belief.

As a country based on freedom of religion (or freedom not to hold to religion), the United States will not abide the abuse of said freedom by any claiming that the right gives them a right to use their religion as a weapon of oppression. Remember your history: the first colonists left England to have the freedom to worship as they pleased. Though they soon forgot the oppression they fled from and oppressed others, their descendants-our forefathers, one generation removed from those who had committed atrocities in the name of religion-had learned and attempted to prevent any future reprisals of that horror through separating church and state and including the freedom of religion within the constitution.

Thus, any religious entity that violates the rights of another to worship (or refrain from worship) in the manner they choose will lose tax exemption and also be expected to amend their behavior according to the Constitution.

All mega churches will lose their exemption. Any institution that preys upon the poor and sells a product, whether it be shoes or the "word of God", is a business not a church. This very act of selling removes any exemption from tax. Like all corporations, these mega churches will have a 90% tax which can be lessened according to the work they do in their communities, their states, and within the country. Any foreign work will not be eligible to be used for this purpose, only domestic work.

The work that will be eligible to go toward the lowering of their tax load are as follows:

1. Delivering food and nonreligious services to the poor, needy, ill, handicapped, and elderly

2. community projects consisting of renovation of buildings. This includes the purchase of materials needed, help offered in the form of workers, meals for the builders, and the establishing of trust between the communities and themselves through restraint and lack of proselytizing.

3. random acts of kindness. Without conditions and without preaching to those you are being kind to. Remember, actions speak louder than words and often times, a kind deed has more impact than any number of words.

4. quit attacking public education. There is nothing wrong with the system, at least not in the manner you present it. You do not need more religious charters, you need to learn how to mingle and be a part of this country.

When you, as an organization, can quit trying to control those around you and realize that your belief is more a personal lifestyle than a political power, you will regain exemption.

Political reform

Both parties will submit to an independent investigation of party policies and methods of doing business. Those members taking money from lobbyists will be prosecuted for taking bribes and lobbyists will be prosecuted for bribery. Both will be charged with corruption and ethics violations. The rule dealing with lobbyist money and lobbyists in general will be amended to eject all lobbyists from legislative chambers and to make taking lobbyist money illegal as bribery.

The only lobbyists allowed in Washington DC will be those that lobby for veteran's rights and the needs of our veterans.

Any politician who believes in war, but does not believe in taking care of the veterans of those wars or the refugees those wars create will be removed from their office and replaced. Any politician who claims to be prolife but deems the poor, handicapped, elderly, widow, terminally ill, black, Hispanic, Muslim, Jew, Native American, orphaned or child to be less than worthy of their service shall be removed from office and replaced. You cannot be prolife without loving all life, no matter the color, creed, age, health, gender, gender identity, or sexual orientation.

As law makers, we are there to do what is in the best interest of our constituents, not just a minority who holds money. We are not there to change the rules and create a religious utopia for those who want to erase the reasons this country was founded.

Any politician who has ties to any hate group will be removed from office and replaced. Any politician who is revealed to be a sexual predator and is to be sentenced will be removed from office and struck from the record as if they have never served. Public service does not lessen the seriousness nor should it determine the sentence once convicted. There is no excuse for such actions and the perpetrator shall be expected to serve full sentence without leniency.

Any politician who wishes to make rights for rapists, or who wishes to make claims that rape does not exist is unfit for office as are those who claim that incest is perfectly fine. Within the context of every belief and philosophy, at least the major philosophies, these two moral wrongs have always been seen as cardinal sins. Any who condone such crimes are unfit to serve as lawmakers and should be investigated heavily. Any politician who calls for drug testing before receipt of government help shall themselves submit to a drug test before receiving their salary. Equal treatment for both representative and represented shall be observed.

ALEC, Citizens United, and all other corporate run organizations and political funding PACs will be disbanded as will the NRA. None of these organizations serve any useful purpose and only serve to undermine the rights of the average citizens.

Political mudslinging will cease. If we cannot stick to the issues and the platforms, neither candidate should be running. What is past is past, and bringing up the past-especially if your opponent has changed their views-is straying from the issues. No using nonissues. These nonissues include:

1. illegals taking away jobs. Currently, most jobs have been leaving the country, so they cannot be taken by anyone except people in the countries where those jobs are headed.

2. Islam being taught in public schools. Last public school I was in taught no such thing. Unless you have stepped foot in one of those Turkish run charter schools and mistook it as a "public" school, no public school teaches any religion. They might research or give an assignment to research and learn a little about a culture and their religion in Social Studies, but no one teaches religion in a public school.

3. fear of a minority or of refugees. Minorities are not a problem. Neither are refugees. As Roosevelt said, "we have nothing to fear except fear itself" (FDR, 1930).

4. loss of whiteness. First of all "racism" or ethnic hatred as it should be termed, is just plain wrong. We are, after all, one race—the human—and are made in a variety of colors, just like flowers in a field. Diversity is what creates beauty. No one is going to lose their color, and even if they did, why are we even worried about it?

5. foreign non-Christian radical terrorists. We have a bigger problem here, stateside called domestic "Christian" terrorists. They congregate under different names: neo-Nazi, nationalists, white supremacists, "militant Christians", fundamentalists, and the KKK, just to name a few. These groups pose a far greater threat to this country and its founding principles than any outside enemy, real or imagined. As for the supposed "radicalized" foreign terrorists, our constant wars have created those in the last twenty years. Stop thinking that they have any bearing on where this country is headed.

6. gun rights. If we were to implement the second amendment as it is written, every gun owner would be expected to serve in the military. Individual gun rights hinged upon the individual's willingness to serve the new nation, thus-if we were to use the original purpose of the amendment-so would any gun owner today. To add to this, no civilian should ever need or desire to own military grade weapons such as an AK47, M27, or any sniper rifle. The argument that certain countries allow gun ownership is a nonpoint, since many European countries expect their citizens to serve in their militaries once they reach 18, as do many Central and South American countries. We are the only country that does not have a compulsory military service regulation or law, making us the only country that does not expect our youth to serve the country as a member of our military. While there once existed a military draft, it was phased out over twenty years ago and military service became an individual choice, except in times of extreme need, which hasn't happened since Vietnam.

7. transgender restroom privileges. Why are we even having an issue with this? My husband has often stated, during the Congressional debates on this nonissue, that he was more worried about the men who were standing at the urinal next to him staring at what he had than he ever was about a transgender. Molesters are not transgender, they are average looking men and women who seem unassuming and who wait for the most opportune time, like when you leave your son/daughter alone in a public restroom thinking they are safe because "everyone is male/female and they wouldn't do anything". This is not, in any way, an attempt to create paranoia where your fellow men

or women are concerned. This is merely an attempt to make a point about who is and is not a possible danger to a child.

8. Homosexuality. In the 1990s, a study was done on why homophobic people acted out violently toward homosexuals and/or transgender people. The result were surprising. 90% of the homophobic people studied were revealed to be experiencing secret homosexual tendencies. The resulting internal battle between their sexual feelings and their rationale made them violent or made them oppressive toward homosexuals and transgenders. While other studies have doubtlessly been performed, probably with the same results, the point being made is that homosexuality is a nonissue and should not be a topic for political discussions or debates.

As a nation, we have had privileges others have only dreamed about. Let us not take our privileges for granted. Let us not make issues out of nonissues.

Taxes to be instituted

Corporate Taxes: 90%

We're going back to the Eisenhower model. It has the following deductions as incentives for growth and equality. The initial corporate (any business with $1 billion and above in business yearly)

1. 10% new equipment deduction for any NEW equipment bought over the fiscal year to create new jobs.

2. 10% growth deduction for any expansion of a business to add more jobs in other towns/regions in the country.

3. 10% growth deduction for jobs created internally, within the business, in attempts to lower unemployment locally.

4. 5% deduction for pay equality within the company

5. 5% deduction for reinvesting at least 80% of all profits back into the business (Top tier salaries do not count as reinvestment.)

6. 5% deduction for employee benefits fostering within the business (again, top tier benefits do not count.)

7. 5% deduction for community involvement efforts.

With items 4-7, management MUST show accurate proof of activities outlined as possible deductions. Though this is same as 1-3, which business owners/heads MUST show accurate and detailed proof, 4-7 are not growth related but rather shows of fiscal responsibility and rely on good ethics and a strong empathy and desire to care for employees.

Tax on the wealthy: 90%

Again, we look to the Eisenhower model for business but convert it to encourage the wealthy to become active in their communities and to compel them to help the economy grow.

1. 10% deduction for philanthropic work (investing in small businesses, donating money to the arts, sponsoring a less fortunate community member's schooling, helping all within a community succeed in some way, donating food/clothing/nonperishables to a homeless shelter. Donating goods to a battered women's shelter/veteran's home/orphanage, donating a portion of your yearly income to a public school/college, etc.)

2. 10% deduction for donating time and labor to community service.

3. 10% deduction for mentoring

4. 5% deduction for promoting community harmony

5. 5% deduction for reeducating through experiencing life in the shoes of another (must be documented and must last more than 1 year)

6. 5% deduction for rebuilding the community's infrastructure.

7. 5% deduction for showing outstanding leadership.

Small business taxes will be significantly lower. (small business makes less than $25 million yearly)

This tax will remain at the current 15-25% but will include the same incentives as the Corporate tax model so that the small business can grow and succeed through being able to expand and provide more work.

Midsize business tax will be comparatively equal to the small business tax with the same benefits. Midsize businesses are those businesses that make less than $1 billion but more than $25 million.

Income tax reform

Income tax should be no less than 10% and no more than 25% for those who make $100,000 or less and no less than 25% and no more than 30% for those who make from $101,000-$400,000. No one, not even Congress, is exempt from this and should be expected to pay according to their income should they desire to have quality schools, roads, fire departments, and other infrastructure. Those making $400,000 and above will be expected to pay the 90% tax expected *from the wealthy. With success comes responsibility to your country and your community.*

All loopholes currently present in the income tax system shall be closed and easement shall be left for those who are of the majority rather than the minority (the 99% rather than the top 1%). Businesses will not have the loopholes they traditionally used to ease their "burdens". Instead, they will be forced to be fiscally responsible and be a positive force in their communities.

Other miscellaneous taxes:

Since there is a growing interest in such things as "Biblical Law", to give Christians a taste of their desire, there shall be the following taxes levied"

1. a hate tax: this tax will be levied on those who preach hate as a "Christian" trait. This will be a 10% tax on all.

2. greed tax: this tax will be levied upon all who preach "Health, Wealth, and Happiness" as a "Christian" way of life. This will be a 10% tax levied on any preacher or religious group caught teaching that greed is Biblically OK.

3. Rape/incest culture tax. This will be a 10% tax levied upon all who preach that rape or incest is OK and is a "Christian" trait.

4. A war tax: This will be a 10% tax levied upon all who preach war upon any culture, color, or country.

5. an oppression tax. This will be a 10% tax levied upon any who think that their religious convictions gives them license to oppress those who are not the same as them or who do not believe what they believe.

6. a "bully" tax. A 10 % tax on all who wish to be bullies.

7. selfishness tax. 10% for believing that God wants you to take everything away from the poor, handicapped, ill, or elderly. Remember: he who stops up his ears to the cry of the poor will also one day cry and not be heard; he who oppresses the needy mocks his maker. (Prov.)

Finally: any church or religious organization that has preached hate, oppression, intolerance, or has been politically active will hereby LOSE their tax exemption. Since you are in the business of selling the "Word of God", you will hereby be expected to pay taxes like any other business. Those that have used their tax exemption as a means to push their political agendas will find themselves heavily fined and expected to pay 20-50 years of back taxes. If they cannot, they will be expected to close their doors and cease all operations in the US.

Religious leaders have a responsibility to preach the word of Christ while also living according to the humility and lowness that Christ instructed you to live. Nowhere are Christians promised a bed of roses or power over the nations, and greed, hate, and fear are all anti-Christian belief systems. Love, Christians, is the underlying message of Christ's ministry. The writings of the Apostles were meant solely for those who believed. They were never meant for you to use as weapons. Acceptance and mercy without judgment or condemnation were supposed to be your hallmarks. One's station in life, one's personal weaknesses, one's personal life, and the color of one's skin was never subject for your approval.

Corporations: If you have the money to give your CEOs a raise every year and if you have enough money to influence politics, you have enough money to pay your employees livable wages and to create jobs. Your responsibility is not to stuff your pockets with your profits, your responsibility is to keep your companies fiscally solvent as well as your employees well-paid. You also have a responsibility to your communities, states, and nation to be leaders, not greedy savages.

Any corporation with more than 25% of its manufacturing outside of the country, or that is an international conglomerate, will be subject to having US citizenships revoked and a foreign tax/tariff imposed upon their goods. This tax/tariff will be dependent upon what percentage of your business is elsewhere. 26-29% will gain 26-29% tax/tariff, and anything over will gain whatever the percentage is in tax/tariffs.

Oil and coal companies:

Your taxes will remain at 99% while you refuse to seek alternative energy options to revert to, slowly phasing out your current source of income to help save this planet while we can, and to ease strain on the ever-diminishing oil and coal reserves. Until you come to the realization that we need to move on beyond fossil fuels, your taxation will remain high so that your profits can help combat the pollution and the negative environmental changes your industry has caused.

Platform on women's rights:

All are equal and have equal rights. It is by the grace of a mother that we are all born. Nine months, they carry us in the womb. Eighteen years, they raise us the best they can no matter whether we are male or female. It is by the love of a mother that we are shielded from most that would harm us; it is our mothers who teach us the most in our youth.

It is a woman's natural right to choose what is done to her body. Just as the rest of us are given a freedom of choice to do either right or wrong, so it is with women. As the equal to men, they are entitled to equal pay, equal rights, and equal status in our society.

Equal rights:

Any self-respecting man or woman also respects their mother. Out of respect, all should see women as their equal. Equal rights means that they stand on equal footing. Rational men see women not as stepping stones or slaves, to be submissive or subjugated, but as equals who are half of what it takes to create the perfect union, the perfect team. Only bullies and insecure men see things otherwise.

Ignorance sees women as weaker and yet it is the woman who bears the weight of the child for nine months and the pain of giving birth, not the man. It is the woman who cares for the sick child and puts up with her sick mate.

She has earned her right to vote. She has earned her right to have equal pay. She has even earned her right to have a choice where her body is concerned. She has even earned a right to stand among her male peers.

Let us establish the following:

1. pro-choice does not , by any means, mean pro-abortion. It simply means that a woman has the choice to make any decision that needs to be made where her body is concerned-whether that is aborting a pregnancy or preserving that life.

2. abortion is not just inclusive to the action of taking an unborn life, but also includes certain other procedures that are known under other names such as the D&C, among others. Abortion is not always an unnecessary procedure, nor are the majority always a choice made by the woman. It is a known fact that a majority of abortions are:

a. the product of the demands of a male who does not want a child and sees his woman as subservient

b. Medical reasons do trump personal desires and, thus, the advice of the doctor must at all times be taken into consideration.

c. Some medical procedures, such as D&Cs, are also listed as "Abortion" even though they are not. A stillbirth and miscarriages are also listed as abortions. Any law dictating "abortion rights" is a misnomer simply because "pro-life" advocates fail to understand the scope of the term and, therefore, seek selfishly to dictate to others what they deem acceptable.

Gun Rights:

As per the Constitution, we the people must fully read the "Right" to bear arms correctly and not just as an "Advocacy" group leads us to read it. We do have the right to bear arms, but only if we are willing to serve our country. "A well regulated Militia, being necessary to the security of a free State, the right of the people to keep and bear Arms, shall not be infringed." The reason for this "right" is made plain. We are to share a responsibility to the protection of this country if we desire the freedom to own arms. These arms do NOT include military grade weapons. We are not at war with ourselves, thus we do not need these weapons on the streets. Nor do we need open or concealed carry, since we are not a third world country or living in the Wild West.

Thus, laws concerning guns will be examined, struck down if unnecessary to the freedom we share, or strengthened if the need is apparent. Restrictions will be placed on those weapons that are not made for hunting or basic self-defense, and removed from any basic armament for everyday life. No guns will be confiscated from law abiding citizens, but will be removed from those who have been convicted of violent offenses committed with guns. Sensible gun reform will be discussed at length. Any organization that impedes the advance of reform will lose tax exemption upon first offense and will be disbanded upon third offense. All organizations must drop all profitable advertising and subsist solely on the membership dues coming from their members. If an organization cannot do this, then they shall disband. NO organization should be used as a front for weapons manufacturers as a means of adding profits to their sales. Any organization found to be acting as such will be temporarily disbanded and not allowed re-incorporation for at least three years.

The time of the lobbyist is over. Now we work for a government of the people, by the people, and for the people. Not a government for the corporation, of the corporation, or by the corporation.

———————

I HOPE YOU ENJOY.

Cordially

Jason O'Hara

———————

SIRS:

The longer you wait to reply, the more hypocritical you appear. Time is of the essence. My own window of opportunity also grows short. This month, the second month of my attempt to form an alliance with you, grows closer to an end.

First of all, let me remind you. I ask for nothing more than your alliance with me. I do not come seeking money. I do not come seeking fame. I come offering you a way to stop things from taking place.

I understand that you are not used to actually taking action. You are used to half-heartedly making little videos that both entertain and try to inform. The problem is that those who need to learn are willfully ignorant...or are too greedy to care. Humility is not found through videos that reveal how "business as usual" is done. Humility, for those who wanted this tax "reform" can only be found through losing it all. Their wealth. Their prestige. Their businesses. Their mansions. Their status.

While I understand that what I propose is not doable with financial backing, I do know that it is doable if one has connections in the right places. Beyond this, I hope I have proven that I can be of other use, especially where it comes to writing and proposing good legislation. sound legislation. intelligent legislation.

I have proven that I have a well-grounded grasp of the Constitution and what is needed. Granted, I need to polish what I have shown you, but that was by no means a finished platform. I attempted to get a little professional help on the Women's rights and education parts, but could not get any interest in forming a solid plank on either. I was getting ready to write a healthcare portion, but never got it started. Life got in the way and by the time I was ready, my only reason for writing the platform had died.

I contacted you because she would've done the same. She sought allies for her run. I seek allies for my endeavor, which she gave her blessing to in her acceptance of the platform I had begun for her. Now is the time, not tomorrow. Today is all we are promised. Today we must do all we can to make a better world. Today.

I urge you to call me. I urge you to make contact with me. Stop ignoring those who could help you. We are all Americans, both rich and poor, and need to work together if we wish to end this nightmare. Otherwise, you are just as guilty (through complacency) as your "Conservative" counterparts.

CORDIALLY

Jason O'Hara

FROM THE DESK OF JASON O'Hara

1209 Filmore

P.O. Box 14

Sidney, Iowa 51652

tel.: 1-712-374-2387

SIRS:

I have given you all the information you need on who I am. I have sent you email after email. I am asking for an alliance.

If you are afraid that I will turn on you after dealing with the opposition, please lay your fears to rest. If you think that I am seeking money from you, don't worry. I am not. Contacts, on the other hand, are much needed. important contacts.

Do I frighten you with my ideas? Progress should scare you because it means giving up old ideas for new ones. It means change from what is comfortable to something unknown.

It means stepping out of a lackadaisical half-hearted, almost cowardly, approach to combatting a problem to all-out confrontation. If we do not do something to stop this now, it will destroy our country. Every little thing that these people get away with tears away at our freedoms, our solvency as a country, and our infrastructure.

I have been proposing to change that. Not through running for office or lobbying, but through other means. I know, to beat the system, you must first join it. But to join the current system also means the inevitability of being corrupted by it. Thus, a new strategy must be brought to bear.

NO, I am not talking about taking up arms. I mean the removal of the secret power brokers, the ones who wrote the legislative scam. The ones who have turned an institution (lobbying) that was meant for government contracts into a way to corrupt and destroy our government. They are not pro-America. But, then, greed is never pro-anything. It is always a source of destruction and has been the fall of many an empire and government. Greed bankrupts. It also breeds hate, contempt, ignorance, and a lot of other negatives.

These negatives give us the type of "leadership" we have currently experienced and are now still experiencing. I am no social or culture warrior. I am a man who has enough insight in business to know that the current business structure is upside down. I understand that the greed at the top (the CEO/board) is what bankrupts a business, and poor leadership leads to failure on all levels. livable wages equal a better income (profit) for all businesses. More demand for products equals a rise in jobs. It is common sense.

At the same time, I also know that to fix the economy, we must also fix the market. WE need to begin to remove the monopolies by breaking them up and begin to add more competition within the market. Competition creates the need for improvement and advancement.

Maybe I have made a wrong assessment here. Perhaps I am dealing with cowards who are too afraid to take a more solid stand on issues. Perhaps I was wrong in thinking that you really wanted to do something about the issue you have been "taking a stand against" through your videos. But, then, maybe I haven't misjudged at all, and you are still trying to assess the sincerity from which I write. Again, I urge you to reply to me. Email me. Send me a letter. Call me. Or do all three. You have nothing to lose and everything to gain.

Cordially

Jason O'Hara

(Jaysen True Blood. Author of *The Vampire Wars: Angel of Death, The Morrow Family Saga, Tales From The Renge, The Badlands Saga, The Hell Patrol Saga, The Daniel Harris Series, The Devil, The Faust Syndrome, Jesus Save,* and many other books)

———————

FROM THE DESK OF JASON L. O'Hara

1209 Filmore

P.O. Box 14

Sidney, Iowa 51652

Tel.: 712-374-2387

Sirs

I am getting the feeling that you were never really serious about your outrage where the tax reform scam was concerned. In a time when all Americans should be uniting, despite their class differences, you are still reluctant at rubbing elbows with a poor man who only wants to set things right for the rest of his fellow Americans. Why? Why are you reluctant?

It would seem, that despite your show of disgust, that you were never truly serious about righting any wrong. You seemed to simply feel that making a statement was all that was needed. Apparently, and in reality, you were wrong. Congress still passes the piece of shit even though you made your voices heard. And you were told that the Republicans did not even care what you had to say. Or even what people like me had to say.

And still, you think that videos are going to actually wake people up. Wrong. Only action will wake people up. Take away their sources of misinformation. Take away the biggest players on the Republican side of the playing field. Reform lobbying s that lobbyists are returned to their original job: lobbying for government contract. Not legislation. Take away the payola that Congress gets from certain industries.

Reform Congressional pay so that they have to work for less, since they spend less time working. Remove the salary and replace it with a wage. Minimum wage. Remove their pension funds and feed that money into the SSA trust, making them have to wait and draw from the SSA fund with all other Americans. Drop their top tier health care and replace it with Medicare/Medicaid. take away their paid holidays and vacations. Take away their paid travel.

If they want a raise, make it to where they have to raise the national minimum wage to do so. If they want better coverage, make it to where they have to give all Americans on Medicare/Medicaid, and ALL Americans in general, better health care. Remove the temptation of siding with for-profit health insurers.

Economically, make it known that we expect Congress to go after the monopolies and break them up. The current corporatist market is destroying the economy and feeding into the current dark economic-political movement of fascism that has seized a minority and the current leadership. The current trend is not a good one. either our economy will collapse, sending you and yours scurrying in panic for the exits, or we will be thrust into a third world war, one which we may not survive.

Infrastructure can only be fixed once the economy is also fixed. The economy can only be fixed by breaking up monopolies and returning choice back to the markets. After all, choice is what drives advancement, innovation, and growth. Demand, not supply, drives the economy through the demand for choice and innovation.

At the moment, I can tell you that there are two wars brewing. On the one hand, we have a third world war. On the other, we have a Second Revolution and/or Civil War. Neither are wars that we can survive from. On the one hand, we face an all out nuclear war because of a madman's pissing contest. On the other, we have hate versus everything else. Neither are anything I want to see in my lifetime.

I came to you with my proposal because I sincerely thought that you were serious about doing something. With each email, I have noticed that your silence, your lack of reply, speaks volumes. It tells me that you were never really serious. It tells me that you have no stomach for a real revolution in thought. You have no stomach for advancement beyond the ho-hum of your semi-serious outrage and poorly acted videos.

Yes, I will continue to email you until I either get an answer, or you are spurred into action. I may not be a wealthy person, financially, but I know I have a lot to offer you in ideas and options. CALL ME. EMAIL ME. Give me a sign that I am getting through, even if it is an angry one because I hurt your feelings.

Cordially

Jason L. O'Hara

Nom de plume: Jaysen True Blood

(author, vocalist, artist, visionary, pioneer of thought, mystic, realist)

———————

(AND THE ONE TO MAJORITY Rules)

Sirs

I cannot afford to send money. I do, however, have a mind for politics, social needs, the law, and business. I could be of great help to you in any of these areas. Please consider me for any position possible, but know that I can be of great help in forming excellent legislative ideas and proposals. I am neither Democrat nor Republican, but am American. I do not play the partisan game, but know what is needed.

Cordially

Jason

———————

SIRS

I find it amazing, and not the good kind of amazing, that you have simply not seen fit to answer me. Do I pose *that* big of a threat to you and your's? Or is it that you deem a commoner less than yourself, and thus, not worthy of your time? Yes. I am intentionally trying to provoke. I want action. I want to be see an alliance between us.

Or is it that, now that you have your tax break, you see no use in fighting for anything anymore? The lack of will shown literally makes me sick. Your half-hearted attempt to make the masses believe that you are even remotely concerned about their welfare literally makes me sick. It is as if you never were interested at all. But, perhaps, I am incorrect in my assessment of your efforts. Perhaps I am looking at it wrong.

Still, it looks more like a diversion tactic than an actual attempt to change things. The more silent you remain, the more I believe that my assessment is correct. Silence is complacency. it is willful allowance and tolerance to what you claimed to be an affront to this country. It makes you look less patriotic than you claim.

In essence, it makes you look as if you do not care about the country or the people who have chosen to speak out...like myself. It is almost as if you believe that only you can ever be in power. Or smart enough to see through the bullshit and lies. But, then, it is your fellow wealthy that propagate the lies. Yes, it is the wealthy on the Republican side who spread the fear and hate through their less fortunate fellows, just as those who back the Dems also seem to propagate enough dissent to put the two sides at odds with each other.

Yes, as long as government cannot function adequately, there is still a reason for the masses to bitch and moan...is this not the view from your lofty perch? Be truthful. As long as there is dysfunction, you still get to be in power. Just remember that the peasants always seem to revolt when they figure out the truth. Can you risk that? Or are you ready to actually make demands for solid reforms and grasp ideas from those down below? After all, you do not know what is really needed down here. I do. I have lived in the lower middle class, and even abject poverty, for my whole life. I know the pain of these people down here. I know the disappointment. I also know that they still haven't put things together and realized that they have been played. But that will soon end if we do not try to fix things instead of marching or making videos. Our time is running out. What will you choose to do?

Will you lay aside your disdain for the common man long enough to join forces with him to effect change? Or will you remain in your lofty towers and your high dollar mansions, afraid that every poor person you see will want a piece of your pie? I have stated, constantly, that all I want is an alliance and some connections inside. With the connections, I can do the rest.

Now is the time to contact me. Now is the time to act. Now is the time to lay aside the class card and work together. As the Three Musketeers would say, "all for one, and one for all." It is now or never.

―――――――――

CORDIALLY

Jason O'Hara

Replies to posts and posts made on FaceBook

the most addictive drug in the world is willful ignorance, which can be distilled down to the harder drugs of hate, greed, intolerance, fear, gluttony, and contempt. These drugs kill more innocent people than any other and keep their addicts from pursuing the truth...which can set them free.

———————————

I STOPPED BEING RELIGIOUS a long time ago. I realized that, no matter how many people I tried to bend to my will, I was still the same person I was. No matter how much of the physical world I despised, my own darkness never ended. I remained the same evil sinner that had sought religion to save me.

Religion does not save. it condemns. Doesn't matter in what name it is formed or what is promised, religion is and always will be darkness. It asks you to judge those around you, those brought to you so that you might learn what is hidden deep within your own soul, as being less than you. It demands that you see yourself as perfect as you are, thus allowing you to remain the same despicable creature you came as. It tells you that you are allowed to condemn the world and that this condemnation will save you.

It lies to you and claims to be faith, but demands that you accept only what your eyes can see and your hands can touch. It flees from knowledge and wisdom, preferring to remain in ignorance and arrogance. In essence, it destroys the "believer".

Notice that I did not say that I stopped believing. I simply stopped being religious.Belief and religion are two different things, just as the spirit and the physical are two different things. Once we realize that our journey is not a physical one, we stop caring what others do or whether we agree with them. We start looking deep within our own hearts and souls to see what we can change there.

Why? Because once you change what is deep within your own soul, your view of everything around you changes. No longer do you see sinners in need of "saving", but mirrors of your own soul showing you what you need to look for within yourself.

———————

FOR THOSE WHO TREAD upon the poor, they shall be poor at some point and be trod upon and wonder why. For me, I know poverty and choose financial poverty over a deficit of compassion and understanding. immigration has ever been the way people move from one land to another through the annals of history. it has also ended the "purity of genes" debate with every migration of the barbaric hordes that fed the bloodlines of Asia and Europe from time immemorial as one empire took another and interbred with the conquered peoples as they spread their imperial wings. For those who turn away the foreigner and stranger, had the Natives been smart and known what White man would do in successive generations, they would have most definitely put an end to the migration (immigration) of English, Spanish, and French as they came to this land to despoil it. Want to play the "illegal" card? Then call back ALL companies which have went below the border in search of cheaper labor, or who have went to any other country in search of cheaper labor. the true illegal immigration is in every single job that is removed from this soil in the name of "saving a penny", which is code for Corporate greed.

———————

(POST)

We are not the only "Americans". this continent is divided into three sections: Canada, the US, and Mexico. Despite the fact that we erroneously call ourselves Americans without including our northern and southern neighbors in that assumption. Yet, there is a growing minority among us who absolutely refuse to admit that there is more to "America" than just the US.

These idiots must have flunked everything in high school and college (if they actually went to College and finished school past the third grade.). they can't even tell when they have been played. Not only did their new "President" play them for fools, but the Republican Party has also played them for fools.

Why do I say this? Think about it. What was the one thing Trump said that he doesn't do, but that a President NEEDS to do to ensure that he/she does not sign the country away to an enemy? Remember, he said that he doesn't read. He even stated that he does NEED to read. Oops, citizens. Guess what? He signed away low FHA rates and your healthcare on the first day. Even worse, he is going to cut Social Security and Medicare by at least half and then doing away with the very safety net the whole nation is going to need after the financial tailspin the Republicans have planned.

And after Ryan and his buddies get him to do these, they are going to turn around and make America believe they are all his fault, knowing that Trump is too much of a walking ego to know not to take credit for the mess that the whole Republican Party is about to make. "But why would they want to do that?" you ask. Well, it's simple. They really wanted Pence in office. Not Trump. They allowed Trump in so that they could appease the Trumpite masses.

So why am I telling you this? Because citizens, you sold your country out just to be betrayed by your own party. Happy landing.

―――――――――

WOLVES, DEER, LIONS, hyenas, and bison, as well as the great and lesser apes, all have hierarchical structures as well. It is everywhere in nature. the problem with the hierarchical structure is that man has been able to corrupt it and abuse his place within it so that it no longer is a natural structure, but a man made thing that little resembles the natural order. not trying to contradict, but there is a manmade structure that mimics the natural order, but does not follow it. where all CAN rise from nothing (many kings did so as did many emperors), there are a select few who oppress and suppress so as to remain the elite through controlling all other structures set to govern.

―――――――――

RELIGION HAS DESTROYED faith, my friend. it is not the structure. it replaces the need for inner change (which is how things around the individual seems to change) with a deep desire to change that which we cannot, the world around us. it has perverted a lifestyle and made it into an oppressive structure based on dead laws (fulfilled by Christ, if you profess) and misread answers we have no original questions for. The Bible is incomplete and is only a beginning point, not the finish line. the truth lies beyond in the world around us in the places we neglect and the people we would otherwise shun. We remain, our whole lives, a student...never truly mastering what we learn because we continually build upon it, add to it. If you simply stop at the Bible, you never reach any stage of maturity. A reliance upon structure leads to arrogance such as that which the Pharisees and Sadducees had. It bloats us and keeps us from being remotely humble (or "poor in spirit" as you so plainly put it). But we must always remain humble and never believe that we KNOW all simply because we proclaim him our savior. I have spent 30 some years of my life studying and re-studying the Bible. Never once did Christ call his way a religion. He referred to it as a way of life. the difference is plain. you implement a way of life, you worship physical rules and regulations and rites and rituals in a religion. Religion allows its followers to stray. A way of life does not. A way of life keeps the individual constantly learning, constantly growing, and constantly challenging each and every aspect of their conviction/belief. Religion just requires that you go to a building once or twice a week to feel as if you are being "a good Christian". But, if it is your way of life, and you are constantly changing and growing within your heart. soul, and mind, you soon outgrow the building and seek to commune with the nature beyond because THAT is where you will find the truth. out there.

I DON'T WANT COMPROMISE. I want advancement, enlightenment, and growth. Hate has no place in this country...or this world. Neither does greed, ignorance, or anything else that impedes the advancement of a civilization. Mankind should be light-years beyond this. Yet, our arrogance holds us back from what we could possibly become.

MEN WHO SAY WOMEN BELONG in the kitchen were never taught how to cook by their mothers nor how to correctly treat a woman in life by their fathers. they were taught, erroneously, that women are the weaker gender. we need to sit all these misguided men in a room, cut a single pie in half right in front of them, then ask them which half is superior. Man and woman are two halves of the same body, equal in every way, incomplete without the other. when the two come together in the correct manner, the two (halves) become a whole in mind, heart, soul, and body.

———————

THE PROBLEM TODAY IS that the institutions that were supposed to teach how to love have fallen to teaching how to hate based off greed, misinterpretation, and selfish bias instead of teaching love without conditions. We no longer have wise teachers, only blind fools leading the blind. We no longer have teachers who can discern, we have entertainers willing to sell the truth according to them. We no longer have followers willing to question what they are taught, we have sheep who blindly follow blowhards who are leading them to their doom. No, there are very few of us left who preach about love and we are the ones called foolish.

———————

THE ORIGINAL IDEA OF a single, all powerful god originated in ancient Egypt under Akhenaten. He raised Atum above all other Egyptian deities and attempted to create a monotheistic empire. Upon his death, Egypt went back to the multi-deity system. God (or El, as he was originally called; ironically, the same name as a Mesopotamian Storm deity), as a singular deity/power is not an original idea. Neither are the laws within the "Ten Commandments", which can be found in the written laws of both Egypt and in the Code of Hammurabi in Mesopotamia. Later abridgments can also be found within the Persian codes and laws of Xerxes and his father Darius, who rewrote the original codes and laws and even added a few.

INSTEAD OF SEEING MANY races, we need to return to the realization that we are but one race, as referred to here. pigmentation, or lack thereof, has ever been a result of climate and the need (or lack thereof) for clothing to keep us warm. As we all originated as a single color, and we all originated in Africa or that general vicinity, we should see each other as a brother or sister, not as a color.

A RE-EDUCATION OF AMERICA has to happen before bigotry ends. We have way too many ignorant people running around stuck in an imaginary past where there has always been some sort of supremacy or "pure race". We are but ONE race, the human race, with many different pigmentations due to climate differences. Purity ended when the the first empire took over a less fortunate foe and assimilated (and interbred with) the population as either slaves or citizens.

DEAR MILITARY: NOW is your time to make a statement and help America. Congress (more succinctly, Mr. McConnell) just refused to pay you. If my bosses refused to pay me to do my job, I would be quite interested in getting rid of those bosses. Please note that it was a Democrat who tried, unsuccessfully, to pass your pay through Congress. this means that the only people left to be mad at are those who seem willing to send you into wars, but hate to pay for you before or after the wars they make up to profit from. The next move is yours.

EARNING IS A NEVER-ending journey. It takes a lifetime to learn all one can, and even then, we haven't even learned all.

I THOUGHT I WAS HARSH with my 25% margin, but my mother (a staunch Republican) told me that my margin was off. She said that CEOs and boards should not be able to make more than 10% more than their lower employees, and their salaries should not raise without a raise in the pay of the average employee. Seems my mother is more progressive than I thought.

WHITE MEN OF GREAT wealth? money and property don't make you wealthy, DT, what you do for others and how you treat those around you makes you wealthy or poor. When will you rich paupers ever learn that? If you are honest, kind, merciful, respectful, understanding, and show great wisdom in all you do, THAT is wealth. Not your worthless scraps of paper and meaningless bits of metal.

I OBSERVED EVERYTHING quietly. I watched as my father and mother had to struggle during the 80's without help (my dad made too much for any form of government aid, being JUST above the poverty line) to make sure I had clothes (my sister actually got a stipend from a relative, so she could afford her own) and school supplies. I realized that the Republican mantra was a bunch of BS. While I don't agree with everything that the Democrats

say, I absolutely abhor the Republican view. Having taken an econ
class, and outsmarting my late wife's government (political science)
teacher on different subjects, kind of opened my eyes on how we
are misled about the economy and the government's role in it. I also
realized that the only way to effect change was to take a stand.

WITH EYES WIDE OPEN, we soon find that we have been kept
in the dark and realize that there IS something laying just beyond
what we were taught to accept.

THOSE UNWILLING TO learn (progress) and thus cooperate
in their own best interests are in a state of decay, not growth. never
be so inflexible as to refuse growth. if you are flexible and accept
growth as a constant (not a one-time deal), then you will always be
able to see that you must cooperate accordingly. to remain blissfully
ignorant is folly, no matter how you look at it. blissful ignorance
leads to the inflexibility we are talking about.

THERE ARE NO SUCH THINGS as failures, only setbacks that
teach us what we cannot do in order to succeed. it is whether we
take the first chance that determines whether or not we are truly
successful or miserable failures. Because it is through the choice to
accept or refuse that we succeed or fail. Not the results of trying.

WHAT I CAN'T UNDERSTAND is that for as long as I can remember, we have always referred to the country as "she" or "her"...and yet, many have been unable to show "her" the respect due a woman. Perhaps it is that male chauvinistic view of a woman being weak that makes them abuse her with their hate, bias, and greed just as they abuse the women in their lives. Why? and why did it take 150 years to allow those used to personify the country to actually vote?

———————

ANYONE WHO BELIEVES that "God" has spoken to them are beyond saving from themselves. All you can do from that point is subliminally convince them that they can all walk on water and wait to see when they attempt it.

———————

Creation is a leftover from polytheistic mythology as is heaven and hell. The early Hebrews were polytheistic. it is evident in the opener where "God" is about to create man. The error is still printed in the Bible as "let US creates man in OUR image" suggesting that there were more than one beings. The NT tries to explain this away by stating that Jesus was there from the beginning. But this is a weak defense for the use of "us" and "our". What gets me is that the OT even records the theft of idols by one of Jacob's wives, which suggests that the "forefathers" were literally polytheistic, but chose a single god to put their full trust in out of that pantheon. This idea would support the use of "El" as the original name of God in the Hebrew texts, thus bolstering the idea that Judaism was inspired by Akhenaten's attempt to create a monotheistic (or perhaps they had adopted his religion, but replaced Atum with El) attempts to unify Egypt under a single deity. Akhenaten failed, but the Hebrews succeeded and led to the rise of Judaism, Islam, and Christianity.

═══════════

YOU STOP DOMESTIC TERRORISM through re-education and/or exile.

═══════════

NEVER TAKE FOR GRANTED. spend every moment you can together because you never know when you will run out of time together.

═══════════

UNTIL YOU HAVE WALKED a mile in another person's shoes, you will never know the depths of their struggle or the heights of their elation when they have overcome. You will only know the cover of the book containing their story.

═══════════

SADLY, THERE ARE AMERICANS who have not learned (or who have refused to learn) history so have never learned from the mistakes of others. They prefer their mythology of superiority to reality and truth.

THE GREATEST DANGER to the economy is not a competitive market, it is unabated greed and unfettered embezzlement of profits.

The Death of Christianity

I HAVE CAUGHT A LOT of criticism for making the statement that Christianity, for all intents and purposes, is dead. This is probably because I say it with such conviction and acceptance that it unnerves those who want to claim that they are devout "Christians". It is meant as a means to make those who hear or read it think.

The truth is that, in the 100 years after Christ's death, man set about creating a physical religion out of something that had been intended as a spiritual lifestyle. Once the physical replaced what was strictly internal, Christianity was dead. In its place stood an institution that seemingly made everything from waging "holy" wars to owning slaves alright. It even seemingly made it alright to hate, seek selfish desires, and judge/condemn one's fellow men.

As a result, the true meaning of all that had been left as instruction, the internal change that had been the full intent, was lost and is now completely ignored. Instead, we were made to feel that waving Bibles and cursing those we feel uncomfortable around was part of our "mission" as Christians. In fact, physical missions came to replace the greatest mission of all: the individual heart, mind, and soul.

Thus, modern Christianity is *not* Christianity. God and Christ have been replaced by idols, golden calves, if you will: ignorance, greed, fear, hate, the Ten Commandments, self-persuits, self-desires for those around us, a trust in physical and not spiritual change, a blindness to our own faults, a blindness to our own arrogance, and even the Apostles of the early church. In a faith where Christ is supposed to be, and is *claimed* as savior, Christ is nowhere in the examples we set. Nor is he anywhere in our learning.

We have replaced him with Paul, Peter, John, James, Jude, or Moses...or all of them. Or we have replaced him with a false message of health, wealth, and happiness that also teaches hate for all who do not believe the message. Why? Is it really that hard to look within to find what needs to be changed? Id it really so hard to realize that those around us only mirror the cracks within our own souls?

Wisdom And Politics

WISDOM LEADS ONE TO back away from both political parties. Designed to divide, the party system is the tool of those who wish to allow us to feel as if we are in control. An understanding, even a rudimentary understanding, makes one realise that the economic ideologies are a bunch of bull shit. The truth is that the markets are driven by demand, not supply. Not by giving tax breaks to people who do not need tax breaks. Not in raising taxes of those who actually have control over the demand side of the market. Money does *not* trickle down. It trickles *up* from the consumer. Only someone who has never actually lived believes otherwise. Politically, we are led by puppets. Paid slaves.

Both sides are bought, even though one side fights, superficially, for the people. Ultimately, they are paid to not pass all that would benefit, but just enough to make the illusion feel real.

The Rich

THE RICH ON BOTH SIDES of the aisle (both Democrat and Republican) are content in screwing the masses. Even though one side states that they are not happy about a tax cut, they secretly seem to revel in it. They tend to throw half-hearted opposition at those seeking a cut, but cease when the cut is passed.

It seems odd that people with money tend to "rebel" through making videos instead of trying to find a better means of getting heard. They want to be seen as benevolent, but lack the will power or the desire to make a concerted effort in actually making a decent statement on things.

As I have observed this, I have come to the conclusion that they all want to rule the country, but none of them actually want to take lead. They prefer to hide away and have others do their bidding. Are these the people we really want to look up to? Are these the people we really want leading us? Or can we do better?

The Poor

I GREW UP AS A MEMBER of the lower middle class. We were so low on the scale that we, for most of my childhood, sat just above the poverty line. I have struggled to rise above my family's status since I became an adult in many ways. For 20 years, I have struggled to find a way to build a business. For 20 years, I have been unable to find that means.

This means that I have always, for all intents and purposes, been poor. Even as I started out in the workforce, being forced to pick up whatever job was available...even accepting less than minimum wage just to make my father happy. Unable to remain with anything for long, and not because I didn't want to work but because I was always the last hired and first let go, I have never had a good work record. When I was married to my first and second wives, they helped me lose several jobs both after I had them and before I had them (the jobs)...keeping me poor.

Every time I have tried to further my education, I have had something come up that put a halt to my advancement. Still, I have not allowed that to stop me. I continue to try.

What I am trying to say is that I understand a bit more about being poor than the majority of Americans, especially those who look down on the poor. I know how it is to live on the street as a homeless person. I know what it is like to watch the jobs in your area shrivel up and head south below the border where the current administration wants a stupid wall. The frustration is real. The risk of dying is real.

None of the rich who are anti-poor have ever had to live on the street. They have always lived in comfort. If they were forced to live on the streets-homeless, moneyless, and jobless...hopeless-they would not survive long. And even if they did, their view would be totally different.

Why Religion Is Obsolete

RELIGION IS THE ACT of putting one's "faith" (trust) in what the eye can see. It incorporates rigid dogma and misunderstood rites and rituals, an incomplete "Holy text" with holes and lacking questions to many answers given, as well as a view that change comes through forcing those around you to capitulate to your will. It literally destroys faith and replaces it with a false sense of belief. Christianity, Judaism, and Islam have all become religions.

As religions, they serve no purpose except as means to further the greed of those who would use religion as power. After all, religion was created by men so that they had power. Control people physically, and you control whether they can grow spiritually. Let faith remain, and you allow them to grow. Allow them to grow spiritually, and the spiritual cannot be fathomed or contained. This makes the enlightened man impossible for the unenlightened man to understand or control.

In an attempt to keep the enlightenment among a small group, religion was created with a hierarchy that put the "more enlightened" above the illiterate and the "less enlightened", thus holding the growth to a minimum within their "flocks". These "shepherds" had they walked according to the "way", would have encouraged both literacy and enlightenment from the very start. For only through learning can one find the truth, and only through truth can one find the knowledge that leads to wisdom and enlightenment.

The act of restricting one's spiritual growth, alone, is reason enough to state that religion is obsolete. Religion is spiritual slavery, binding the "believer" with the chains of dogma and rigid doctrine while demanding that they oppress those around them with their misinterpretations and mistranslated verses, their ill-considered judgments and damnations, as well as their lack of any real knowledge due to the lack of discernment. This set of more alarming symptoms are more reasons to consider religion obsolete.

True faith is not a religion. It is a way of life, just like Buddhism is a way of life. It leads one to the truth, thus setting them free from all bonds. It guides one to be tolerant, kind, loving, understanding, compassionate, truthful, trustworthy, and less interested in physical wealth and happiness. And the rewards are greater than anything one can find in the physical world.

A need to return to faith, true faith, is also a reason to see religion as obsolete. Morality is not found in a book. Neither is compassion. Or true love.

Only by doing away with religion can we remove the power of those who twist the truth into lies. Only by walking away from the institutions that preach hate and violence will we advance to the next level of consciousness. It is time for us to walk away from the rigidity that controls so that we can become what we were intended to become.

The Two Party System

THE TWO PARTY SYSTEM, while it works great on paper, is the easiest system to corrupt. The wealthy only have to choose a side to fund and they can wage their wars against each other through political wrangling. Hell! The average citizen believes anything the wealthy say!

Want to create hysteria over an ethnic group? Call them "illegal aliens" or "undocumented refugees" and tell the masses that we have too many filtering into out country! The people will riot in the streets! Want to control both government *and* the religious community? Claim that one party is for "Christian" values and get the more radical in religion to fall in line.

Want to start a war? Spread fear and terror throughout the country by creating a "terror organization" to keep the Middle East unsettled and to threaten our allies so they HAVE to rely on us. Nothing like a good war to push profits through the roof. And, of course, if you want to control how people read the Constitution, just twist it so that it reads as if they have no responsibilities for the rights they have been granted! Buy,buy, buy! It's all for the profit of a few!

Want to control the economy? Deregulate so that only a handful control the market through thinly disguised monopolies, yet tell people they "have a choice". Yet, push out any small business that comes along that might prove to be competitive enough to give you a run for your money. Want to control the people? Take away their jobs, then blame a minority as you are taking those jobs to countries where you can get away with paying peanuts...or just plain automate so you can cut down on the number of actual employees you have to pay. But always blame those who have nothing to do with it. That way, no one suspects you or your greed.

No, the two party system has outlived its purpose. Now, it is just a machine that does the bidding of two different sides in an ageless war between rival aristocracies. The only difference between the two sides is that one actually has a few rogues left in it that want to do good while the other openly lies and doesn't care that it lies. Still, the two-party system, and the money machine it feeds off of, is obsolete.

The only way to fix it is extensive reforms that may not actually do any good. That leaves only one recourse: to abolish it and reform the whole government, weeding out the outside monies that keep good from being done, while getting the bad passed and into law. This would also entail a complete overhaul of the media so that opinion is relegated to a super small section of media time, political neutrality is of the highest priority (no more seeing media as right or left) and only the facts are discussed—without a spin.

A vast deprogramming and reeducation of the people must also take place to lift the illusions of the puppet masters. This means that all would be expected to take a short course that gives an overview of how the government is supposed to work, what the Constitution *really* says, and the views of our founders. It also means that there needs to be a revocation of all tax exemptions given to mega churches and televangelist, as well as any radical groups that think that they are entitled to run the government. We need to purge the hate, greed, and divisive from our midst and rebuild. Bigger. Better. Stronger. And willing to learn from all mistakes made throughout history. The first mistake learned from is the formation ot the two-party system.

Family History

I recently learned that I am a distant cousin to the royal family. This isn't just the case on one side, but both. They diverge at a certain point, but come back with the marriage of my mother and father.

To clarify, my mother's family is linked to the Gruffydd (Griffin/Griffith) Royal house of Wales, the The Scottish royal house of Stewart (which, incidentally links me to the Bruces, Rosses, Campbells, and Wallaces), and the Plantagenet family (the ancestors of the current royal house) as well as the more recent royals in the 1400s and 1500s. Her family is linked into the Hamilton family (yes, *that* family), but through Alexander's uncle.

The main family, the Sparks family, whose surname was derived from the word "sparrowhawk", was a King's knight and at least five served as mayor of London. Some of my ancestors were Knights of the Garter (a special order of only 5-7 who were the Queen's Knights) and the vast majority of my ancestors served as members of Parliament. Even the father of William "The Pilgrim" Sparks was referred to as Sir.

On my father's side, I am also linked to the English Royal house, but also to The Henry family (yes, *that* Henry family). I have yet to actually make the correct connection, but am pretty sure that she was an unnamed member of either Patrick's offspring or of one of his older brothers.

Some of my ancestors proved to be very rebellious, fell out of favor, or fought here in this country for our freedom. And that spirit led subsequent generations and members to fight in the Civil War, and other skirmishes throughout history. I suppose this is why I am a bit rebellious myself. It is genetics.

Creative Writing Lessons

———

Lesson 1: World Building

For this exercise, keep in mind that each lesson is related. Lessons 1-3 will be used in lesson 4, "the rough draft". After the rough draft is finished, I will proof and edit the work for initial grammar/spelling errors as well as run-on sentences and repetition.

These will not be graded, but please make sure you do your best.

Lesson one is in two parts.

<u>Part one</u>

Build a simple world based on the world around you. As you build describe different aspects of the world you build. These aspects should be as follows:

Who peoples your world?

What kind of creatures live in this world?

What is the layout of your world?

What is the main belief of your world (IE science, magic, monotheism, polytheism, etc.)

What are the main industries?

What kind of government?

This part should be notes only.

PART TWO

Build a more complex world using the information from your first world. Flesh out every aspect so that the world that results is as close to 3 dimensional as you can get. Leave no stone unturned and no leaf uninspected.

SUGGESTION:

For fun, build several (3-5) worlds for your files. Most authors will build upwards to 10 different worlds as they write, storing those they are not immediately working with on paper or in files for later stories. Some authors (myself included) tend to work on at least 3 stories/books at a time. Not all of these stories are in the same genre. These are known as Works In Progress (or simply WIPs) also remember that diversity is good when writing. Never work in just one genre.

LESSON 2: CHARACTER Building

Characters, as you already know, are the most important part of your story. They are the source of action. They drive your world. Although some stories do well with one or two main characters, the vast majority have a host of main characters and supporting cast. Again, this lesson is divided into two parts.

Part 1:

Come up with 3-5 main characters, those characters that will be present throughout the majority of your story. They do not have to be in order of importance, they just need to be written down. As part of this exercise, write down a complete description of each. As with world building, building a detailed description of your characters will help you in the structure of your story, solidifying and strengthening it and making it more linear and coherent.

Part 2:

Come up with as many supporting characters as you possibly can. A maximum of 10 should suffice. For those you name, write a short bio. For the nondescript/unnamed (town cryer, constable, etc.), write a brief description of them and their duties in your world.

Note: many authors will make several of these lists for each WIP they plan on writing, and even sequels of earlier works.

LESSON 3: PUTTING IT All Together, Part 1

Now it's time to begin putting it all together. Well, sort of. One od the most common ways that writers plan out a story is through a brief summary. This summary serves as a plot line that they follow. While some authors use outlines, in fiction, the art of outlining doesn't always work. This is why many have decided to write brief summaries (which, Ironically, can double as your blurb on the back of your book) instead. With summaries, you have freedom to stray away from less solid ideas in favor of something totally different.

I chose to have you write a summary because of this fact. Now, put your world and your main characters together. At this point, do not worry about your supporting cast. They aren't important yet.

Write at least three different possible summaries incorporating your world(s) and your main characters. Remeber, this is a summary, so it should only be anywhere from 2 paragraphs to a page, depending on how detailed you make it.

If it helps, and you are looking at making a multi-chapter (or book length) story, feel free to number the chapters according to chapter

Note:

I rarely write more than a short paragraph, but for the purpose of this exercise, I recommend that you write more just as practice. You're going to need it for the next lesson.

LESSON 4: PUTTING IT All Together, Part 2

Welcome to the most exciting lesson! This lesson is where you take the summary you just made and turn it into your rough draft.

At this point, you have several (2-3, maybe more) different scenarios on how your story can unfold. I want you to choose 2 and write stories based off these summaries. Make them as wild, following your summaries, as you want...but make sure they do not end the same.

If you had multiple paragraphs, you should end up with as many chapters as you have paragraphs. The point is to expand each paragraph so that it is a chapter, adding to them as if each are tiny stories within your story. If you are writing a short story, a chapter can be anywhere from a few hundred words to around 1000 (I try to keep a uniform 1,000+ words in each chapter, but I don't always reach the count I hope for.)

The rough draft serves as a rough idea of how your story is going to look. There is no reason to strive for perfection here, just to get the story written. Mistakes and plot holes can be fixed later. Right now is about getting the story fleshed out and ready to proof and edit.

Chapters need not be numbered. They can have titles. But if you feel more comfortable, go ahead and use numbers...but there is no need for "Chapter" to precede it.the shorter your chapter/chapter head, the more appealing it will be for your readers.

One last thing: don't worry about your audience and what they will read. Write for you. You are the creator of that world and those characters. Once the story is done and in print, there will be people who will be drawn to it.

LESSON 5: PUTTING IT All Together, Part 3: second draft

So you have finally submitted your rough draft to an editor and it has come back with correction marks and recommendations for changes. Some of these will be grammar/punctuation marks, others will be where there are plot holes, and still others will be marking/suggesting changes where there is repetition.

Do not despair. Grammar and punctuation are easy fixes. Perhaps you used the wrong word, or you misplaced a punctuation mark.

Follow the suggestions given, unless you are in the right (some editors are anal when it comes to commas, sentence lengths, or paragraph lengths. I am not. Since I write in a manner that gives my characters character, I would be an editor's worst nightmare.)

Plot holes are where something is left out. Generally, these omissions leave big unexplained areas in your story. Suggestions on fixing plot holes will be in the form of a question (who? What? Where? When? How?) and will point to ways of closing these sometimes embarrassing omissions. Or there will be a request for you to add what is called "backstory" orthe story on how the character(s) reached their current predicament. Never include flashback scenes unless you have a backstory to explain the flashbacks. (It was pointed out to me in my romance *Long Cold Winter* that my flashbacks had no backstory and were slightly confusing. The result was *The Morrow Family Saga*. I submitted a short story to the legendary Piers Anthony, who rarely critiques stories for others. He sent back a brutal critique that helped me create the prequel. With *Angel of Death*, I originally started with book 7 and had not intended to write a series. After a suggestion from a late author friend of mine, I started the story with *Dreams I'll Never See* simply because I needed a backstory.) backstory is the biggest plot hole you will run into. Try not to start in the middle of a story. Always try to start at the beginning.

Repetition is a disaster waiting to happen. 'Said' is overused in writing and speaking. For common words, seek synonyms or other ways to express them. This includes every action. Some stories work well with an indirect way of indicating the action of communication. Others do not. Be creative with your word usage.

Foriegn Policy (Definition/Description/Discussion)

FOREIGN POLICY: HOW we view, treat, or react-as a country-to other nations. The policy behind the amount of diplomatic attention given to a foreign country.

Military policy: Ideally, the policy on how we, as a country, base our military spending on. If we sway to the defensive side of the spectrum, spending is supposed to be based upon a less aggressive policy. If we sway to the aggressive side of the spectrum, we base military spending on how many wars we believe we can win and how many lives we are willing to expend in our aggressive push to conquer and control. The moderate, or middle ground, is a balance between aggression and defensive ideals where neither side outweighs the other. This moderate ground tends to build as if it is in defense mode, but at a slightly higher rate to accommodate the possible needs of an offensive response to an attack upon the country.

Foreign policy, ideally, has nothing overtly to do with the military policy though the two tend to be linked through the security needs of our foreign embassies, our bases abroad, and the idea that a global marketplace gives us the right or need for a militarily driven foreign policy. Foreign policy, of and by itself, should never be driven by military might. Diplomacy should always be the core of foreign policy, driving us to settle disagreements, mediate, and represent ourselves in a peaceful and nonaggressive way.

There should never be a corporate land grab option in foreign policy, though trade should be a key and central motive. Control of areas, acts of war and aggression, and greed should never be a part of how or why we hold a certain foreign policy. War, for the sake of war or profit, should never be a part of foreign policy either.

Obama's foreign policy, or "the Obama Doctrine" as it was called, was based on a less aggressive and desire to preserve as many American lives as possible while resisting getting into too many wars we could not win. He based, and rightly so, his policy on the ideal that the best action we could possibly take in the Middle East-and elsewhere where there was strife-was to slowly withdraw from those areas and allow them to solve their own problems or to gain an agreement through diplomacy, not war. This policy gained Obama much criticism from both his staff and the opposition when it should have gained him bipartisan support since the majority of Americans were desiring the return of our soldiers from Afghanistan and the Middle East where they have been enmeshed in disputes that we have both caused and become a big part of.

<u>Foreign policy vs. Military policy (to be used in my government classes for my Foreign policy post)</u>

Foreign policy is driven by diplomacy and treaties in an attempt to prevent future wars. Through treaties, accords, and various agreements, alliances are made and peace obtained. By its very nature, foreign policy is not connected to military policy even though there is a certain amount of military involved in diplomacy-usually in the form of embassy security or bases in foreign countries to fulfill defense agreements-acts.

By their very nature, trade agreements are a part of foreign policy but the act of global goods takeover is not. Neither is the act of giving away jobs to countries that, by the very nature of their monetary system, offer opportunities for "cheaper labor" or "cheaper goods". Corporate warfare has nothing to do with diplomacy and, therefore, cannot be looked at very kindly. Manufactured wars, wars based on faulty or manufactured intel, and war for the sake of war are not a hallmark of a healthy foreign policy.

True foreign policy seeks to bring peace through mediation, not war due to differences in belief, governing style, or color of skin. It does not thrive on the desire to wrest control of natural resources from their rightful owners, the desire to control foreign banking systems, or the greed of a minority.

Different types of faulty and misguided foreign policies:

Nationalism: the ideal that a single ethnicity is better than another. This ideal is driven by a minority within a country (IE white corporate leaders, rich white idealists who have no real knowledge of real life, etc.). This form of foreign policy usually appeals to supremacists, especially when combined with imperialism and isolationism. The reason for this appeal is due to the idea that, in theory, you can cleanse your country of "unwanteds" while waging war on other countries to gain both land, slave labor, and natural resources. Examples of this mixture of ideals can be found in 1940s Nazi Germany, 1940s Fascist Spain and Italy, and the movement of the Alt Right of today.

Imperialism: a drive by the corporate sector to force conquests in attempts to divide and conquer other countries so that they might either control the people or the natural resources thereof.

Isolationism: the idea that a country can sequester themselves from the rest of the world and be better off after doing so.

"Divine Right" or manifest destiny: an ideal that is related to imperialism, but is infused with a touch of nationalism. The idea that a country has a right, given by "God", to expand upon land bordering their own. This usually entails the mass extermination of those seen as more savage or inferior.

Military policy is not related to or connected with foreign policy in any way. While the military budget does cover security at foreign embassies, and that budget is controlled by Congress (not the State Department or Secretary of State), it has nothing to do with our country's foreign policy. Military might does not equal diplomatic action. In a healthy foreign policy, military policy remains at a moderate level. This means that development and training is not heightened, as it would be during a time of war, but remains at a slightly lower level—as it would be for a defensive military policy, but with a greater sense of a need for advancement in technology and training in that technology. This does not mean that the training of new recruits is slowed, just that spending and the need for spending is lower.

In a defensive military policy, the focus is maintained on defense rather than aggression against other countries. Attention is given more to a buildup of arms and soldiers for defensive use and steered away from the intent to invade, raid, or cause instability in a country or region. An aggressive military policy is focused on the intent to invade, raid, or cause instability and not on defense while a moderate military policy is primarily focused on defense, but see a possible need to send forces abroad as a line of defense/

offense that aids in the overall outcome of a possible attack. It also realizes that military action is only used when diplomatic avenues are unsuccessful and an actual attack is made upon the country or its people.

Obama's foreign policy attempted to create a healthier foreign policy that tried its best to refrain from warfare, while attempting to solve problems through open diplomacy. Heralded by some, it was also opposed by many—including some among his own party who supported the cause of war despite a lack of agreeable intel to corroborate the need for military action beyond the use of a few drones (which had been signed for by George W. Bush shortly before he left office.).

Comparison of the Different Ethical Philosophies

Nonconsequentialism:

Act-no general rules, just actions/situation

(Joseph Fletcher)

Strength: left up to individual

Weakness: left up to individual

Divine- God(s) set forth the rule/action, rule/action is right. Not defined by self-interest/other interest but on "higher power"

(John Calvin)

Strengths: strict moral guide

Weakness: unfounded source (historically proven to have originated in other sources)

(Bible, Koran, Torah)

Intuitionism-any well-meaning individual already has a sense of right and wrong

Strength: well-meaning individuals try to do what is good

Weakness: well-meaning does not always mean good outcome.

(Austin Fagathey)

Rule- there are or can be rules that are only the basis for morality.

Strength: rules are presence

Weakness: even if the rules are a basis, they don't necessarily apply.

Kant's duty ethics- nothing is good in and of itself except good will regardless of interests or consequences.

Strength: defines human nature

Weakness: denies any existence of guilt or innocence without a prevailing factor (good will) or lack thereof.

(Emmanuel Kant)

Categorical imperative- asserts that an act is immoral if the rule that would authorize it cannot be made into a rule for all human beings to follow.

Strength: sets forth a precedent

Weakness: limits to can/can't moral judgment.

Practical imperative- cost-benefit/end justifies the means

Strength: something is right as long as the end is justified by the action.

Weakness: can be misinterpreted to allow any action from killing without cause to unabated greed.

Prima facie- a form of duty ethics, name means "at first glance". Duties which all must follow except in certain situations.

Strength: connects all to a list of "moral duties"

Weakness: allows for exceptions.

(Sir William David Ross)

Consequentialism- concerned with consequences to actions

Strengths: serves as a definitive what's right/wrong through cost/consequence

Weakness: rigid reliance on reward/consequence.

Ethical egoism- what's right for the self

Strengths: promotes self interest

Weakness: does not take into account the interests of others

(Epicurus, Ayn Rand)

Care Ethics- men and women are different when it comes to ethical decisions, but equal.

Strengths: puts men and women on equal but different grounds

Weaknesses: Kohlberg's study was inconclusive, not taking into consideration the moral teaching of the children he studied while gathering their answers; Gilligan's theory tends to be unclear in whether it raises women above men or sets them on equal footing.

(Carole Gilligan, Lawrence Kohlberg)

Utlilitarianism- what's good for all/the majority

Strengths: takes in consideration how actions affect others

Weaknesses: omits the self

(Jeremy Bentham)

Virtue ethics- inborn, character-based, born of responsibility

Strengths: focuses on character, not rules, as basis as long as the act furthers the common human good.

Weaknesses: does not see actions as good or bad in and of themselves. Limits factors

Flood Control

=====

<u>Design for flood control idea:</u>

Levees line almost every inch of Iowa's river systems. Traditional levees are not efficient at holding floods back.

The new design would have an outer wall (facing the river) of reinforced concrete of reasonable thickness to hold both structure and be able to hold back flood waters. This outer wall would have intakes embedded into it, 1 set every mile, a set containing four stacked intakes—the fourth being at or below water line.

The interior would be wide enough to accommodate the pipes needed to transport the water to the settling tank and on to the turbine as well as a service space for inspection and repair use to ensure that the pipes remain in serviceable condition.

The intake/transport pipes for bottom intake port should be placed in such a way that water will flow correctly to the tank (in non-flood times, the tank should be no more than half full, allowing it to fill when in times of flood.)

All intake pipes would lead to a "settling" tank where the water can remain still enough for sediment to settle. Ideally, there should be 3-4 tanks, the majority for flood season where the need would be great. These tanks could also be used when the main tank needs to be cleaned.

There would only be 2 -4 small/medium hydro-turbines per station. If 2, then there would be 1 reaction turbine and one impulse. If 4, then 2 of each. The reaction turbines would run continuously, providing energy in average (and drought) years while the impulse turbines would be utilized as flood waters built pressure.

Flood Control Proposal

Traditional levee systems are ineffectual, at best, against flooding. Armed with this knowledge, I set about researching probabilities on remedying this problem. each time, I came to the same conclusion.

One solution to the problem at hand is to hybridize the levees to contain diversionary slues to hydroelectric turbines. The concept is to have powerhouses set one every mile, with the one at the five mile marker set to be a constant generator. The intakes for this powerhouse will be devised in such a way that they will allow water to travel to the power house even during drier seasons. The other four powerhouses will be set where the intakes would only allow flood water to be carried to the powerhouses.

The runoff from these powerhouses would then be transported to a water treatment station/plant to be treated for mass consumption.

Problems to be solved:

1. a study of the current levee system and whether it is possible to convert, even a small section (50 miles) to accommodate the concept.

2. development of a compatible turbine system

3. placing the water processing/treatment facilities and development of aqueduct to carry runoff to facilities.

4. Acceptance of idea by surrounding communities

5. Acceptance of idea from state and local governments

6. contracting the work.

I am currently in the research and development stage and waiting on feasibility data. I am planning on meeting with emergency management personnel (the director of county emergency management) and whoever else I am directed to on this.

Economic systems and the political structures they tend to attract

Communism: Communism, an economic system that states that the collective owns all and shares equally (the basis of the hippie communes of the late sixties and early seventies) tends to attract the authoritarian political structure. Communism isn't concerned with who leads or government in general. The idea is that the collective governs equally with no one leading or having all the power. Yet, the economic system tends to attract the abusive power drain that is the authoritarian political structure. Authoritarians tend to control everything from aspects of private lives to the market which is supposed to be a collective, not government controlled.

Socialism: socialism is often confused with communism. Though similar in structure, there are stark differences. Where communism is about the collective being equal, socialism is about social responsibility and helping all be equal in the economy. Socialism also tends to attract authoritarians, though there are many socialist democracies. This system is a socioeconomic system which combines the need of the society with the economy.

Capitalism: capitalism is often confused with corporatism, but the two are drastically different. Capitalism thrives on a free market system where entrepreneurial efforts are rewarded with success and the government regulates the market just enough to stimulate competition and economic growth. Most capitalist countries are democracies, though some are monarchies or other government structures.

Corporatism: corporations monopolize the markets and greed runs amok. In a corporatist economy, there is no real government regulation. Corporations are allowed to monopolize the market, leaving no room for entrepreneurs to add to the competition. The instant any form of competition is presented, the corporations find ways to put it out of business, whether it is through a buyout or through price gouging. This form of economy is usually found in countries that have Nationalistic governments such as Nazi Germany of the 1940s, fascist countries, dictatorial governments where corporate money can keep the leadership bought due to corruption and collusion. A few formerly soviet countries have traded their authoritarian communist economies for an equally authoritarian corporatist economy.

Business/Economic Proposal

Farmers control the prices and own a stake in the company; the community also owns a stake in the company. This makes both community and farmers equal partners in the success or failure of the company.

There will be a set salary for board of directors. This salary will be permanently set at between $100,000-$400,000. The idea is to start all at $100,000 and gradually advance them to the maximum of $400,000 over the tenure of the board. This board will consist of a CEO (to be selected from the young [high school age: 15-18] entrepreneurial minded population and trained in how to run a company) the board will be chosen from those who invest from both farming and private sectors (the local community). These positions can be handed over to family members should the board member decide to retire. Another way to look at the management is to think of it as family owned and family operated.

Labor wages will be set above minimum wage ($20/hr or more) to set a precedent and shall not drop below this.

Products: all organic foods. Organic meats, vegetables, soups, dairy, cereals, etc. packaging will be alternative sustainable packaging. Plastics will be based from vegetable starch; sustainable paper/cardboard will be made from corn husks, corn silk, and corn cobs. Ink will be soy ink.

Farmers will be able to diversify their crops, rotating yearly to optimize their yields and their profits. Farmers control the prices of their crops, setting an agreeable/affordable price for both company and farmer.

The products will be sold both locally, in-state, regionally, and nationally competing with nationally known brands to reintroduce active competition in the marketplace.

Known facts:

There are only a few major companies in food distribution, of these are Conagra, Kraft, Heinz, Post, Kellogg's, and Nestle. This is not a balanced market. Even the generics do not add enough competition. What is needed are more companies that can offer a more national/international push to competition both in the prices of produce and in competitive pricing on unprocessed resources (in this case, produce from crops and beef/pork etc.)

The lack of competition allows for a company (or set of companies) to produce substandard foods/products without need to improve or to set fair prices.

The illusion of choice is due to the consumer's lack of knowledge on what monopolistic company owns which sub-brands. For instance, a company that puts out several brands of peanut butter will give the illusion that the buyer has a choice even when they are purchasing goods at the local store.

A buyer who believes that Peter Pan is better than Jiff are fooled into a false sense of superiority when both brands are owned and produced by Conagra Inc. Just like those who swear by Orville Redenbacher and put down Act One or Vogel's, all three popcorn brands also owned and produced by Conagra.

Another way of looking at it is from a car buyer's dilemma. As we know, there are only two major domestic car companies: Ford and GM. A person who swears by Ford, but puts down Mercury has no clue that both brands, and therefore all makes and models, are made by the same company just as a person who swears by Chevrolet but hate Oldsmobile or GMC has no clue that they are damning a brand that is nothing more than a sister to what they swear by.

It is a proven fact that we live under this illusion of choice, not knowing that we really don't have a choice. By building the company proposed, there will be more competition in the marketplace and a representation of the state on a national level.

What is proposed:

Soup, steamed vegetable (frozen vegetables, steamed vegetables, soups)

Cereal production

Ice cream/creamery

Organic butcher/meat supplier

Sustainable paper/cardboard manufacturing

Eco-friendly plant-based plastics manufacturing

Soy ink manufacturing

Organic bakery

In return, the community, county, area, and state will see a rise in revenue and help the national economy.

While I understand that results will take time to become apparent, I believe that the project will be extremely successful and benefit all involved.

Business and working 101, part one:

A lot of good ideas never make it as businesses because those who begin a company based upon that idea give in to greed. Whether embezzlement or through raising salaries at the top before there is ample room for such an action, greed makes otherwise sane entrepreneurs do insane and extremely stupid (and unethical) things. They will break the rules, break laws, even steal from Peter to pay Paul (take what is earmarked for one bill to pay another).

Theft, by any other name, is still theft and greed by any other description is still greed. Both go hand in hand. A person who is in the business solely because of their greed will steal customers from a fellow rep within their group, invade the privacy (by looking through another person's "friends" list on social media-Facebook, Twitter, etc.-looking to see who they can poach as a possible customer) seek out weaker-or people they see as weaker-people to make into targeted reps they can cannibalize (poach entire lists of customers and potential downlines from), and basically carve out nonexistent territories that they supposedly "own". They make poor leaders and even poorer business associates. They are the ones who end up destroying every company they work for, but never see themselves as the cause...only the victim.

A business guru once said that if you are in business solely for the sake of greed, you are in business for all the wrong reasons. In fact, greed is never a good reason to have when going into any venture. It destroys both personal and business relationships and makes the one consumed by it unhireable.

Innovation, passion, vision-these are the true reasons you, as a representative, should be in business. You should be there because you love the products. Even more, you should be there because you want others to see just how enjoyable those products are and because you want to share your passion. In fact, your passion for what you represent should be in how you speak and how you carry yourself.

Even the worst salesman could sell someone a skunk if they are passionate enough about it. If there is a passion, it pours out from literally every pore. It sets a glow and makes you seem more self-assured. Before you begin, ask yourself three questions:

1. Do I love the products?

    With this question, you should have first begun your journey by making purchases first and trying the product. If you have not, then you can't really have a passion for the product. You can only have an interest. The two are not quite the same. Buy what you are thinking about selling first. Try it. See what it does for you. If you love it, then sell it. Experience is the best way to sell anything.

1. Can I make others see how much I love the products?

If the answer is yes, then you have the passion, drive, and potential to reach whatever goals you set.

1. Do I have people I can share this with without appearing to be pushy?

    Family, friends, business associates (if you work a "day" job), and even professionals who are in your life (doctors, dentists, teachers, etc.) are all potential customers. The key is not to push. Casual conversations can often lead to a sale, but you must let them lead. They will either show passing interest ("Oh, that's nice") or active interest ("tell me more"). Either way, do not press. Let them command the conversation. Let them be the ones to decide. Do not pressure or coerce.

Those who choose to be in business because they believe in a product will nearly always succeed. Their positive attitudes and friendly demeanor will nearly always win out over the greedy, pushy attitudes of those who only see the monetary advantages. Those who allow their greed to be central to their reason for going into business rarely, if ever, believe in the product. They only believe in their need to feed their greed.

<u>Business Proposal for bookstore, short form</u>

Proposed owners, Jason Peterman (to be referred to in future as Jason O'Hara) and Kelly O'Hara, propose to buy remaining stock from original owners and seek out a location for new store. The new and used books from the original owners will be sold on consignment until none are left.

A small portion of the store will be reserved for best sellers from mainstream publishers, and these will be in limited quantity, according to local interest. The remaining space of the store will be devoted to children's authors, independent YA authors, and local/regional/national independent authors of all genres. Erotica will have a very limited area, but will also be included.

Also to be integrated into the store is a music department, which will highlight local and national independent musicians as well as a department devoted to independent film. Other activities related to music, literature, and the arts will be integrated piece by piece as expansion allows for it.

Jason Peterman is better known to independent literature as the author Jaysen True Blood and has written books ranging from science fiction and fantasy to horror and even historical fiction and drama. His current projects are *The Morrow Family Saga*, a historical fiction series that will span from 1950-present; *Faces In The Crowd*, A drama series placed in the present; and the *Angel Of Death* series, a dystopian/vampire series.

He has been in writing for nearly 20 years, professionally, and has been a published author since 2007. His poetry has been featured, from time to time, in anthologies from Poetry.com since 1992. He has one song, which was published in 1992.

His published works include:

Seven By Jay: Seven Short Stories

The Price Of Lust: Book One Of Faces In The Crowd

Angel Of Death: Dreams I'll Never See

Angel Of Death: Waiting For The Sun

The Morrow Family Saga: Hand Me Down World (book One, 1950)

The Morrow Family Saga: Do Ya Miss Me Darlin'?(book eleven, 1960)

Long Cold Winter

Whispers In The Spring

The Faust Syndrome

Jesus Saves (not a Christian book, a suspense novella)

A Month Of Thanksgiving

Mexican Radio And Other Short Stories, Volume I

Mexican Radio And Other Short Stories, Volume II

The Price You Pay And Other Short Stories

So Here's To Twilight And Other Poems

He is waiting for covers for books 3 and 4 of the *Angel Of Death* series as well as for the follow up to *A Month Of Thanksgiving*. Also in the works is book two of *Faces in the Crowd* and book two of *The Morrow Family Saga*. He has also been working on a single Christian fiction novella, but has yet to finish it.

He is also a recorded vocalist and songwriter and experienced businessman.

Kelly O'Hara is Jason's fiancée and life partner. She is a fulltime student and versed in the legal side of things. She is also an aspiring children's author and sole inspiration for Jason.

Business Plan for Twice Told Tales Books and The Fox's Den Music and Movies

Phase one of the "Pepperbox Publishing" division of Diversified Arts and Enterainment

History

The plan for Twice Told Tales/Fox's Den grew out of a need for a venue from which independent authors, musicians, and film production companies could sell their books within small communities. Add to this my background as an independent film, book, and music reviewer and you have a store that is run by someone who knows a good book when he sees one, knows good music when he hears it, and knows a good indie film when he watches it. Along with this, I am also an author and musician myself, so am active in the publishing world.

While Amazon sells indie products, they do not focus solely on these. Anyone can buy products from Warner Bros, Universal, MGM, and Fox as well as any of the major traditional book publishers. Most who go to Amazon are there to see if their favorite movie has come out on DVD, to find the latest book from their favorite author, or to see if their favorite band/artist's music has been released yet. The indie markets are mostly seen by those who seek out unknown authors, musicians, or film companies.

This leaves sales of indie products to those whose products they are. Promotions and advertising are solely the responsibility of each author, indie publisher, production company, and musician. Thus, there is a need for a brick-and-mortar bookstore that deals solely in independent productions.

In my original business plan, I had intended to build stores last. But upon studying my ideas closer, I realized that the store should be first and everything should grow from that. As an author, I know how hard it is to do one's own promoting and advertising. I also know how hard it is to get your materials into a major chain store.

The idea is to start small and grow, not to start big and spread out. With this in mind, I began business classes. Armed with this knowledge, I will be able to operate a business without any problem. Initially, I was going to start an online store from which I could grow the b&m store, but with a few setbacks, I was unable to open the store online.

Linked to this store, and its eventual online sister, are three blogs: The Radio-Pirate Presents (indie music review blog), Dark Portal Reviews (book reviews), and Dark Fantasy Independent Movie Reviews (film/television)—all of which are on wordpress. These serve as a platform to help authors, musicians, and film companies gain promotion through reviews. This promotion is free of charge, I simply ask for a CD, copy of book, or copy of DVD so I can review them. I have done these reviews for over ten years.

Since inception, I have been afforded the opportunity to buy out and re-open an established (but closed) store, the original Twice Told Tales, which I am keen on taking on. From this, a new TTT will grow that serves mainly independent authors and attached to this will be The Fox's Den where indie music and film will be a predominate feature.

Layout

The main store will be a book/Cd/film store. Also included will be a café/snack bar where customers will be able to get treats or something to drink. The plan includes homemade snacks ranging from pepperoni rolls, cinnamon rolls, etc. as well as homemade ice cream. Along with these, the customer will be able to buy a cup of coffee, a smoothie, or a cappuccino while they rest in-store or browse.

The store will be divided into four sections. It is planned that the snack bar/café will be centrally located with the books on one side, music on a second side, and film on the third.

All selections will be independently published or produced. Books will be from indie authors, music from indie musicians, and film from indie production companies. Traditional publishers and productions will be special ordered when requested.

Management bios

Jason Levii O'Hara was born Jason Levii Peterman in 1974. He is a published author with 10 + books to his name on Amazon. He writes under the pseudonym Jaysen True Blood. He is also a recorded musician with three finished songs available on CDBaby.com, one of which is available also on Amazon.

Currently an Entertainment Business student with Full Sail University, he hopes to build an entertainment company of his own.

Kelly Ann O'Hara is Jason's wife and life partner.

Main Competition

Barnes & Noble- the most trusted name in booksellers. Their market share mainly focuses on traditionally published authors, but they publish a select number of indie authors through their Nook Books. Most of these are e-books, but they have started a small venture in POD which has impressed a few authors. Still, their reach is limited so they do not pose much of a threat to TTT.

Traditionally, the two biggest bookstores were B&N and Borders. When Borders folded, this left B&N as sole major retailer. There are a number of smaller bookstores, but most have niche customers (IE history, science, writing, reference, bargain books, religious books, classics, used books) Most offer recognizable names among their authors with very few independent authors.

Amazon- Their online store sells every indie author next to traditionally published authors. Their POD is basically free for any small author, leaving the author's funds for promotion purposes. Still, with the millions of choices available, many deserving authors do not get the sales they need or deserve.

Walmart- Authors have to distribute their works through the distributor that Walmart uses to buy books,

CDs, and movies. This means that the author often has to pay a fee to be considered which is often too expensive for small struggling authors. This leaves most indie authors out of luck where Walmart is concerned.

Other brick and mortar bookstores tend to lean toward traditional publishers. The excuse I have heard is that many small presses and indie authors are "too expensive" to carry much from. This is something I know to be untrue, since a typical book, through amazon, ranges between $5.75 and $8.98. These are books published through their POD services (CreateSpace) and include those books published through an indie publisher (any author is free to use a publisher title). The only exceptions to these are "Vanity" publishers such as AmericaStar Books, Vantage Books, etc. These books can range between $15.00 and $25.00, maybe more, per book.

Still, the idea that indie books are more expensive is a fallacy that has been used to keep many exceptional books from being sold nationwide.

Break even statement/corporate structure

It is my intent to ensure the welfare of my future employees through paying all the same salary. Since I will make an income from royalties off my own works, I shall not take a salary once the store is fully operational.

All will receive a salary/wage starting at $15/hr. There are plans of offering health benefits and a retirement/401K plan at a later date, once the store is able to do so.

Proposal for Action Figures

Action figures to begin the series: Cris Juarez (The Angel of Death), The Creeper (villain), Voodoo, Grady (werewolf)/Grady (man), Angel (technowizard)

Cost per action figure: Approximately $80,000

Cost includes: creation of molds, materials, safety testing, development, and cost per 1,000 figures.

Brief description:

Action figures are characters from the series of Dystopian/post-apocalyptic Vampire novellas *Angel of Death*. Cris Juarez is the main character, the story is told by her. she is four years old when the series begins and each book is spaced twenty years and covers 300-400 years. The main plot is Cris's mission to search out and destroy the mysterious Sabbath Stones and to kill the lord of the Vampire Nation, Jason Kalkolides.

There is a possibility of a "child" version of Cris, but at the moment, the adult Cris and The Creeper are the only mockups ready to go into productions. Voodoo, Grady, and Angel will soon join the collection as my artist is working on the mockups of all characters.

There is extreme interest in these action figures and I could possibly be able to raise a portion of the funds simply through pre-orders.

The breakdown:

- 6" Action figure

- 5,000 toys of one character

- Timeline: 7-8 months

- Freight: to the U.S.A.

Costs included:

Unit Price: $10 - $10.50 per toy

- Production Setup: $25,000

- Creative Services: $5,000

- Safety Testing: $2,500

- Freight: $3,000

The unit price being $10-$10.50/figure would create the need to retail the pieces at between $11 and $13.50 (average price for an action figure in the stores) I would, as the vendor, have to add an additional $5.50 for shipping and handling. But this, alone, would only cover the cost of the action figures themselves, not the production costs which include freight costs, packaging design, and ensuring that the figures meet safety regulations.

Human Potential

———

It is a known fact that humanity only uses up to 15 or 20% of their total brain. This leaves so much potential to unlock. I love movies that explore this. *Lawnmower Man* was the very first movie I saw that dealt with this. *Lucy* also discusses this probability.

But what *if*? What if we were to find a way to unlock the 85-90% of our brain that is unused? What would be the result? What new powers would we have? What new abilities? Would we be able to fully unite with the universe?

The questions are endless. The potential is infinite. We might even overcome death should we find a way to utilize the rest of our brains. Or even disease. Or every ill that besets mankind.

Perhaps it is time to begin the next jump in evolution, the next set of adaptations. Along the way, we might be able to realize exactly what we were being told in ages past. We might even be able to visualize and accept the path we have always been meant to take as humans.

The Possible Outcomes of Reaching Our Potential

———

1. Telekinesis- the ability to move things mentally
2. Telepathy- the ability to read people's thoughts and even control thoughts.
3. Teleportation- the ability to mentally transport oneself from one place to another
4. Psionic powers- psychically manifested energy powers (the ability to control fire, water, electricity, etc.)
5. Unaided flight
6. Time teleportation- the ability to transport one's self back into time
7. Shapeshifting
8. Transcending this physical existence.

Though there are infinite possibilities with this, this gives us a good idea where things could begin.

Biocybernetics

━━━

A fictional technology I created when I was writing storylines for comic books I planned to publish in the 1990s. I had a pretty awesome artist who was doing the art for me, but the comics never materialized. Still, in a few of my more recent science fiction, you will find references to it, especially in the upcoming *Return To Zero* series. Of course, you will have to read the series to find out exactly what happens, so won't go into that here.

Biocybernetics is exactly what it infers. It is cybernetics (robotics built to replace human limbs, or to enhance/correct organs such as the eyes and heart, for example) specifically created to bond with, enhance, and even be slowly assimilated into the human body. It relies on nanotechnology to bond and assimilate, with allowances for every possible obstacle that can arise during the assimilation process.

A key to its success is that the DNA of the recipient is used in the formulation for their specific biocybernetic implants. A biocybernetic arm would use the DNA of the recipient to create the networks, structure, and microchips to be used in the implantation. This allows the recipient's body to recognize the new additions as a part of the body and begin bonding with it.

Think of it in terms of forming bones, skin, nerve tissue and muscle tissue through extracting a certain amount of a person's DNA, then implanting those tissues-in the form of a preformed arm or leg-onto where they had lost an arm or even a leg but with a set of microchips that enable the new limb to bond and become a natural part of the recipient.

We have the rudimentary technology to create this new technology. We even have the ability to perfect it to a point where we can use it in everyday medicine. All we need is the innovation and innovative minds to pursue it.

Cloning

Cloning presents a definite promise. While I am not totally on board due to ethical questions, I can see the possibilities. Cloning organs. Cloning limbs (see "Biocybernetics"). Cloning ourselves.

Perhaps, in the future, we can even clone out the imperfections. And even the evil. Then, again, perhaps not. What will actually define future limits on this? Or will there be?

Volunteer Colonization and Forced Exile Beyond Our Solar System

We have ever been colonists. From time immemorial, we have migrated and colonized lands. In many ways, it makes me wonder if we actually originated here. Especially the way we gaze at the stars wistfully and long to be "out there". And if we did not originate here, then that means that we were never meant to remain here for long.

It is my strongest belief that we are meant to colonize space. When is a question, though, since we have not been that kind to this planet and should learn to respect Earth before we go elsewhere. We have the technology. We have the spirit. We have the drive.

We just can't seem to learn from our mistakes. We can't seem to get away from the greed. Or the hate. We can't quit abusing our planet.

But we must. We must decide what is most important in order to get to the place where we will be able to leave and begin the colonization process. We must rise above what we are to become what we should be. Then, and only then, will we be able to leave this planet to see what is beyond.

The question that remains is this: Should we exile those who are incorrigible beyond our system? Or should *we* be the ones to leave the planet, leaving it to them to destroy or save? Which should be the first to leave? And how do we make sure that we do not fall back into the same routines that have brought us so close to self-destruction?

If we exile, we should make sure that they cannot return. We should also make sure that they cannot stop anywhere in this system. They should be given everything they need. Terraforming equipment. Supplies to build settlements. Hydroponics to keep them fed until they have their new home fully terraformed and able to bear crops.

If we leave them behind, we must ensure that we leave no technology we have advanced behind. Leave them with just the basics. We should take with us samples of all life so that we can breed it in captivity and create a new stock.

Thoughts on Creation Mythology and the Creation Scenario in the Bible

———

Mythology is a corruption of possible clues to our origins. I lump the Bible in with mythology because, the more I inspect it, the more I believe that the stories hide a less fantastic history that stretches back farther back than we choose to believe. Matching both ancient myth with the Bible, we find many similarities. ;aced throughout both are words of wisdom and clues to the true origin of humanity.

I do not believe that the creation scenarios are literal creation. Especially not the scenario in the Bible. In many ways, it tends to resemble the beginnings of a colony, or even a pair of colonies. Perhaps the colonies formed an alliance, intermarried and grew, eventually sending out more colonies. Or, perhaps, other colonies already existed. Or the two original split into four, four became eight, eight became sixteen, and so on.

It is even a possibility that the two original continued to divide into more colonies. This would certainly explain the proliferation of named and unnamed "children". It would also make a little more sense. Please realize that these colonies did not have to be very advanced.in fact, if the original colonies were already in a state of decline, it would make perfect sense to de-evolve a little, losing advancements already known, as the early stages are in progress (sort of like if we were to send colonists to the moon or Mars without a supply line or the know-how needed to continue the technological advancements needed to press ahead in the lifestyles they are used to on Earth) due to the lack of knowledge on how to manufacture certain known advancements. Thus, any and all advancement would be lost over just a few hundred years. After a few millennia, a colony, or the resulting civilization, would simply collapse, leaving the beings to de-evolve more until they began utilizing indigenous materials to build the rudiments of new cities, then relearn many of the less technical abilities such as music, simple art, and even tool making.

This "Eden", namely the planet, that they have found eventually steals away their ability to advance as they were already advanced upon arrival, but had none skilled at the technologies known. Without the knowledge, technology died and along with it, the first civilization. As humanity forgot its past, it began to keep record in the form of oral history. From this would be born the rudimentary mythology that would form to create a rich tapestry of hidden history and illusory misrepresentations of actual places, people, and things.

Man, being as absent minded as he is, lost the vast majority of his own history, keeping only bits and pieces of the mythology that were important for "explaining" nature. Mesopotamian mythology was, then, recycled into (or implemented into) an emerging new "nation" of loosely confederated tribes that were leaving Egypt. The monotheistic system by which they were now being shepherded was a remnant of Akhenaten's attempt to "unify" Egypt under a single deity (Atum) whom the now numerous Hebrews (later to be called the Israelites), a branch from the Mesopotamian peoples of Ur, Whether by leave of the Pharaoh, exile/expulsion, or by war, the Hebrews migrated from Egypt into Sinai.

Ironically, the push to reform a polytheistic nation into a monotheistic empire worked for the Hebrews who were able to remain monotheistic for centuries. But this does not change the fact that they took the name of a storm god as the name of their own, or that they used the terms also used in the worship of Atum as well as a few other Mesopotamian deities(King of kings, Lord of Lords). In fact, this moniker is attached to the main gods of every people from Persia (though this became a title used by Xerxes when he took on the man-god persona) to Greece and Rome.

The monotheistic worship of Atum would be the root from which Judaism, Islam, and Christianity would spring. It would be twisted further by Rome to become a darker religion in an attempt to hold all power over their quickly waning empire.

Thoughts on Floods in Mythology/Bible

―――

While I believe that the flood myths actually record something important, I do not necessarily see it as a flood. So many speak of a ship floating in the air above the flood waters rather than in the waters themselves. Could we not be talking about a possible journey through space to escape some catastrophe? Could the 40 days and 40 nights not be counted as a metaphor for 40 generations or a possible millennia?

A nearly two month flood is rare. Almost unheard of. Even in the Mesopotamian region, specifically, the Tigris/Euphrates River valleys in what is now Iraq and Iran. The average flood spans at least three months, six at the most, from onset to final day of dryout. This means that the 40 day count (even in miracle terms) is a bit too short...by at least 40-50 days.

And the collection of animals, the eclectic mix of humanity, and all is absurd. What if humanity had not been sinners, and the flood had actually been a last ditch effort to save it from a cataclysm so great that a metaphorical flood was used to describe humanity's escape from where they originated? What if the 40 days and 40 nights was simply a way to shorten a journey that took light-years and the Ark had been a ship that lifted off from one planet and brought mankind to another safely?

As humans, we read everything so literally. We accept everything we read, especially myth, legend, and incomplete histories as

Gospel truth when they are not. It is fatal to read something as literal history when there is nothing to support or dispute it.

It is my theory that humanity did not originate here. Earth became a temporary refuge from which we have never left. The flood scenario is actually misplaced in the grand scheme of things and misworded so as to make it seem in the correct spot. I believe that the "Flood" scenario came first, leading to "The Garden of Eden" scenario, which is also a misrepresentation of what actually happened. "Eden was the original name for Earth, a refuge that offered much, including the very mechanism that would cause our predecessors to devolve into a lesser being, then scatter to the winds giving rise to various adaptations from the negroid features (probably near the original if not the Middle Eastern/ Mesopotamian), Caucasian, Indigenous, etc.

Post diluvian "Eden" mentions Babel, where mankind supposedly divided through "God's" intervention. Though Babel, or its ruins, exists, perhaps the divine intervention was not so literal, but rather, perhaps the city grew too large and many sought lands further away. Or, perhaps, Babel and its tower are a metaphor for what is really hidden within the creation myth only using a city and a tower reaching towards the heaven. Or, perhaps, in one last effort, before the fall of man was complete, he tried (in vain) to return to his home among the stars through the building of one special city—the tower being the ancient way of describing a rocket.

Abram, Sarai, Israel, and Egypt

————

I find the modern Christian's explanation of the narrative of Abram absurd. According to the Bible, Egypt was already an established empire. Archeology has proven that Egypt enjoyed being an empire for many millennia, maybe even stretching back before Ur and the rise of Chaldea. Though this supports the narrative, it does not support the modern Christian's explanation. It takes at least 100 years for a solid kingdom to form. A kingdom can consist of 1-10 cities. But Egypt, as described in Genesis is already an *empire* of great size and immense wealth and power. This would mean that it would have had to exist for at least 500 years, but most likely for a couple millennia.

Ur, being the center of Chaldea, had been at its strength for at least 100 years before the tale of Abram and Sarai. Chaldea collapsed long before the fall of Egypt, just to give the magnitude of Egypt's size, strength, and wealth. From Chaldea would rise Assyria, The kingdom of Akkad, the Canaanite city-states, Babylonia, and Philistia just to name a few. Also to rise out of the ashes of Ur and Chaldea would be a small nation known as ancient Israel.

So the age of Egypt, alone, is enough to refute the modern Christian's claims that the Earth is only 7,000 years old as Egypt had been around for at least a couple millennia (also destroying the time count from "Adam and Eve") to rival Chaldea.

Skip ahead to the whole "Israel coming out of Egypt" scenario. The scenes described in Genesis and Exodus that deal with this speak of the Pharaoh enacting certain precautions because he was afraid that the Hebrews would rise up against him and take over his throne. In order for a small group (12 to be exact) to become large enough to become a threat to a powerful ruler, there has to be at least 500 years or better between the original 12 man group and the resulting "nation". I say at least 500 because a ruler (governor) named Joseph is mentioned for at least 500 years in early Egyptian histories as a wise and noble man. After 500 years, he vanishes from all record as does mention of his family. This is replaced by a record of a growing population of "foreigners" within the country who have been there for 400 years. These foreigners are seen as a growing danger and unwanted.

Theoretically, I would place the exodus of the "Israelites" from Egypt at about 1000 years from the death of Joseph and his brothers. This would have given the group enough time to become large enough for the decrees on killing babies to be a warranted decree in the eyes of a Pharaoh who doesn't remember Joseph or how these people's predecessors literally helped keep Egypt alive during a drought that devastated other kingdoms, causing them to collapse. It also adds credence to the possibility that the Hebrews took notice of Akhenaten's short lived attempt to create a monotheistic empire.

At the same time, this also begs the question: what if the "Israelites" had actually been those Egyptians that had taken to Akhenaten's monotheism and had been exiled because of it? What if the actual exodus had been of a religious faction that threatened the Pharaoh's power? A religious faction that had secretly grown to become almost the size of a small nation? Makes one kind of wonder. Or, perhaps, Akhenaten's reforms had been in an attempt to bring

Egypt under the interlopers' "God" through equating him/it with Aten (Atum) and he failed.

The truth of the matter lies not with the actual wording, but within the story itself. Strangely enough, there is history (or myth) missing in between so that there is no way to fully realise the actual event. Was Moses actually a disgraced Egyptian noble who headed the remnants of the religion of Aten (Atum)? Was the Ten Commandments a distilled version of Egypt's own laws, in the form of Akhenaten's reforms, with a few laws from Hammurabi's code added for safe keeping?

Historically, it has taken centuries to build a nation large enough to be seen as a threat to a host nation. It took Rome's predecessors centuries to unite or conquer the tribes surrounding Rome. it took them centuries more to become the tour-de-force they became as an empire. It took the birth of Alexander of Macedonia to create the Greek "Empire" even though it fell with his death. That was 1000 years or better from the rise of the city-states. And, yet, modern Christians believe that the Earth is 7000 years old, despite mountains of archeological evidence to the fact that the Earth-and the existence of man and civilization-is much older.

The Old Testament

I am a student of history. It is where I find much of my inspiration for the books I write. I am also one of those people who search for solutions to problems that traditional measures inadequately try to prevent. I observe everything and see the fallacies in all things. Politically, I am probably more progressive than most progressives. Ethically, I am less inclined to be corrupted or swayed away from a belief in the common good.

I pay attention to advances made by archeology that help prove or disprove histories, whether written as a record, or included in "Holy Books". I even seek out sites like http://www.reshafim.org.il/ad/egypt/history18-20.html/ for confirmation of plausibility of many of my theories and thoughts on certain histories.

It is my best guess that the "Israelites" first arrived in Egypt during the First or Second Dynasty in Egypt. This would have allowed the small tribe of 12 brothers to grow into a large enough subgroup to threaten the Pharaoh's power. An educated guess would be that they intermarried into the Hyksos, who would have been regionally related (if indeed the Biblical account is accurate...but I question that notion), on numerous occasions to keep from intermarrying their own until actual blood relation was diluted enough to warrant it. Over the millennia that passed between the 1st/2nd Dynasty and the 19th Dynasty (Ramses II), enough time would have passed to allow the creation of a small (but separate) "nation" within the Egyptian empire that would draw the attention of the Pharaoh. The time frame would roughly be 3100 BCE-1227 BCE (roughly 1,873 years). Upon this, we can believe that even a small group can grow large enough to threaten the leader of the nation they reside in, even if that existence had been peaceful. It is also more than enough time for a ruler to forget the benefits the predecessors of the people in question had brought.

Yet, Sumer, the land in which Ur was located (now Iraq), had a far older civilization (dating from before 5000 BCE) that may or may not have predated Egypt, since very little is actually known of the protodynastic period of Egypt...which would have been around the same time frame, give or take a millennia. China, whose known rise began in 2,000 BCE, also began its emergence from obscurity. We must realize that Greece would begin building around 3000 BCE (est. 2900), but would not reach its zenith until 321 BCE. Rome would appear around 753 BCE.

So now that we have mapped out the timeline for civilization, let's look on back-following the Bible-from that point. We already have civilization being 5000 years old (at least) at the death of Christ. But this does not figure in the supposed beginnings of man. It only follows civilization, or what we know of it.

In the Bible, Adam supposedly lived 930 years. This is nearly a millennia. It is also, conspicuously, the life of Rome as an empire give or take a few centuries. During those years, he and Eve supposedly had numerous sons and daughters. Of these, only a handful are mentioned. The first of these are Cain and Abel. like many who call into question the accuracy of the Old Testament, much of which literally copies Mesopotamian and near eastern mythology as well as a bit of Egyptian myth and lore, see plot holes everywhere. Holes like *who did Cain and Abel marry since they were adults when most of Adam and Eve's children were still babes?* Or *why does it sound as if the whole beginning of man was one big incest orgy?* Questions like these led me to believe that the OT, from creation to Abraham, was myth and not history. After all, how do you explain to a nation how man originated on Earth? In fact, I would wager even the flood is myth.

Abel died as an adult, but murdered. We are not told how old he was, nor are we told whether he had any children. We are left to assume that he was a bachelor when he died. Cain is not mentioned after his exile so we are left to assume that he never died at all (imagine that). We are, however led to believe that, from Cain on, the men married their sisters. But we aren't told that there were any sisters their age."Sisters" don't come along until after the first boys become men of great age.

Generation after generation live to a great age, producing a multitude of children, and die. The lineage literally reads like a coded record of cities that rise and fall over time, not like a blood lineage. This makes me wonder if the myth is actually a record of city-states or settlements rather than the generations of a family. It would seem to catalogue the rise and fall (or the division of) cities and city-states as the settlers searched for a more arable land to cultivate and become numerous in.

The flood seems a bit out of place where it is recorded. Could it be possible that this piece belongs at the beginning of the collection to explain *how* humanity actually arrived here? Could it be that it was shifted because those in control of the tribes did not want the truth to be revealed? Or maybe it got shifted by accident and was never returned to its rightful place.

The account of Babel seems to describe a city where they were attempting to build a rocket or a ship so that they could leave Earth. Perhaps they realized that they were never supposed to remain here. Or maybe they wanted to see what lay beyond. But the "tower" sounds suspiciously like a ship, a rocket, so that they could leave. Whatever the answer, they must've disagreed on the finer details and we are left to wonder exactly what happened next even though the division is attributed to "God".

So now, we have covered at least 5,000 years of prehistory as covered by the Bible in myth and legend. This brings us to the beginnings of Sumer and the city of Ur. Ur was the home, supposedly, of Abram and Sarai (later Abraham and Sarah). It is here that the histories pick up once again on the lineage of "Adam". It also follows through with the births of Isaac and Jacob and on to the 12 boys that would become the supposed patriarchs of 12 tribes.

Abram, or Abraham, could have been a real person. I am sure that most of his story, though, is probably a myth made to give a people purpose and a "divine calling" as they left Egypt (or fled) and began their rise to power. Whether Isaac existed or not is neither here nor there. Apparently there is some truth to his story, because Jacob is mentioned briefly (though by an Egyptian adaptation of his name) in the records of Joseph (also under the Egyptian version of his name) from Early Egyptian records. But we do know that Joseph did exist. He is recorded in early Egyptian writings as a wise and powerful leader who aided Egypt in a time when the world around them was suffering drought. He disappears from all mention in Egyptian writings 500 years before Ramses II (the Great), giving a little credence to the story told in Exodus, though the whole slavery thing has been proven by archaeologists -at least where the pyramids are concerned-to be a total myth.

Many of the events, the "miracles", of Exodus are questionable-save the Red (Reed) Sea flowing backwards or parting. This has been recorded at the same time as a volcanic eruption was recorded in Greece, proving that the "parting" could have simply been caused by seismic activity, not by a "god" causing the waters to part. Still, for a mystic or priest wanting to control those he is leading out of a land they had grown accustomed to, the use of the divine is a wonderful tool. Moses, as we are told, was a magician of great power—though the authors rewriting the histories are sure to attribute his power to "God".

Most of the happenings in Leviticus, Numbers, and Deuteronomy are most likely myth. The Sinai is a well-travelled trading/invasion route of the age in which the "Exodus" supposedly took place, though the Hebrew people do appear as a loose kingdom a few hundred years later. We can be fairly sure that I and II Samuel is a legend retold, but that from I Kings to II Chronicles is fairly true, though a bit abbreviated. We also know that the events in Esther did actually take place because they are also recorded in the histories of Persia under Xerxes. We also know that the "prophets" did exist because they appear in the records of the empires under which they were subjugated, though they were of minor interest. In the eyes of a true Christian, the Old Testament is basically null and void, having been fulfilled by the birth, life, ministry, death, and resurrection of Christ making the demand for capitulation to the 10 Commandments anti to a Christian's journey and mission.

New Testament and the Modern Christian

For the most part, history according to the New Testament is fairly straightforward. Though there is no actual proof of Christ's existence, even in Roman records, the basic lessons he supposedly taught can be found in nearly every system of belief. They are the true core to Christianity, the true fundamentals. It seems strange that only four books cover his supposed existence and that he is not mentioned at all in Rome's records (someone as important and as controversial as him would have definitely gained the emperor's attention).

I am not calling into question the validity here. I am merely stating fact. Rome always kept records of those who were seen as a threat to the emperor and the empire. Where Christ is concerned, there is no such record. Either he was not seen as a threat, or he was so localized that they ignored him...which seems so unlike Rome and her emperor, who noticed when anything was out of place in Judea and had a large presence there.

What I am calling into question is the validity of what a growing number of "Christians" are believing. After all, the letters of Paul, Peter, John, James, and Jude do not contain the questions to which they contain answers for. They allude to, but never quote the question (IE they state in answer to your question..., but they never state what the actual question was). Thus, these, as guides are ineffectual and incomplete and should not be seen as valid for points on much of anything (though Hebrews is beautifully written, but undervalued). The Revelations, also, should not be seen as a guide to much, since "prophecy" (fortune telling, but "Divine" in nature or appearance) tends to be in images we hardly understand from a modern perception.

Thus, in essence, the Christian should only see four books out of the whole Bible as a guide. But the modern Christian seems to have turned their back on Christ altogether, seeking instead the fulfillment of their own biases and their own desires. They have abandoned the truly spiritual nature or the message for a set of physical idols that can gratify and justify their biases and their lusts.

Dimensions, Time Travel, and the Universe

I recently saw a video where a young child described perfectly what my theory of the universe has always been. Since, I have seen a second of yet another child who explained it in a similar fashion. Perhaps there is a growing awareness that the universe is not as we perceive it.

Dimensions are as infinite as the measurement of the universe. Each dimension is an alternate version of every moment in time. Perhaps they are also the source of our fiction. Infinite stories, playing themselves out waiting for an author to "discover" or "create" them, a memory or residual memory that appears in the form of written word.

I have often wondered what the repercussions of jumping from dimension to dimension would be. Would it cause the infinity of dimensional layers to collapse? Or would it simply alter each dimension because you were there?

Time, at least future time, is connected to dimension since the future is never certain and has infinite possibilities. This is why the only possible direction to go is backward. Yet, going back would also alter the present and possibly the future. Especially if we went with the purpose of changing something that happened to an individual or to change a single event. Yet, just the act of going backward, if only to observe and record, would not actually alter anything. Only by changing events would we change the past, present, and/or future.

The universe, connected to both dimension and time, yet separate from both, is also infinite. Yet, I believe that the universe is divided into divisions called Microverse, macroverse, multiverse, megaverse, maxiverse, ultraverse, and the ulimate—universe. A microverse, like the universe, is what we see as the universe, though a universe is made up of all the microverses put together. A macroverse is many microverses combined; multiverse is many macroverses combined; megaverse is many multiverses put together...and so on, until you have the universe, ever expanding into the infinite void. Each microverse is a mirror image of its sisters, a realm unto itself, where life may have been placed on other planets rather than on Earth and perhaps they are what is known as dimensions, thus making the concept of dimensions incorrect as we know it.

Author's Note

As an author, I have learned that one must always learn, and one can only learn through research. And more research. And the more you research, the more you find that will oppose what you have been taught as true, making you (hopefully) question the validity of what you have been taught, and why you have been taught that fallacy. As an author, I have always been an avid student of mythology and have often found the parallels between myth and the Bible to be uncanny.

And as I have evolved mentally, I have also learned to remain abreast of all new archaeological findings that support history or oppose popularly held beliefs. New and exciting finds have always inspired me in my writing as well as in my search for the truth. The more I learned, the more I grew. And I still grow.

I found people like Edgar Cayce, Aleister Crowley, and many others fascinating. I also found different systems of belief to be the same. Moreover, I have always had a fascination with the spiritual realm and human potential.

The selections in this book are original ideas. some have been submitted to engineers for review, others to political organizations for review, but none have actually been published in book form until now. Some selections are readily found on FaceBook as both my own posts as well as answers to post made by others.

A few of the subjects are results of story ideas, others are from years of research and meditation. The Presidential campaign platform contained here was originally for my late wife who wanted to run for President in 2020. I was more than willing to help her get to where she wanted to go in her career, but sadly, she didn't to last Thanksgiving (2017). She knew of the flood control idea I had, as well as the economic idea. She was an ally in my own vision as well.